The LOST Episodes:

Curb Your Enthusiasm

VOLUME #2

Ray DiSilvestro

&

John Miller

Dedicated to the cast and crew of Curb Your Enthusiasm, with special acknowledgement to Larry David, for his inspiration, encouragement and guidance.

MOST IMPORTANTLY,
a special thanks to all our fans. Without their encouragement and support, Volume 2 wouldn't have been possible.

Extraordinary appreciation to Jonny DiSilvestro for his input and creative contributions for the following episodes: FunkHouse, World's Greatest Asshole, and The 'G' Spot.

Table of Contents

READ ME FIRST. Trust us, it gets better....

This page is *still* boring (see: Volume 1)...but trust us, it gets better, **MUCH** better. If you've read Volume 1 of The LOST Episodes, you can skip to EXODUS - Chapter 1. (*If not, why not? Go to Barnes & Noble, or Amazon.com, or Walmart.com and purchase a copy.*)

This book is written in a style that alternates insights and narrative of its development with script-like outline-episodes of a sitcom. The sitcom we wrote mimics the style of the HBO comedy series, Curb Your Enthusiasm. The original 'Lost' episodes (Volume 1) were not so much 'Lost', as, 'Never Found'. Volume 2, on the other hand is more of a transition from 'Lost' to 'FOUND!'. Our original intention was to put together a few samples of our creative abilities to showcase our talent (again, Volume 1). Creating the material was EASY. Volume 2 follows up with our placing the finished work with the right people and getting it produced.

Originally, we (John and Ray) started out writing a generic sitcom. As it grew into multiple episodes and eventually, multiple seasons, we found that generic character names were difficult to follow and identify with. Ultimately, as a tribute to one of the people that inspired our writing, the material we created follows a format similar to that used in the production and filming of Curb Your Enthusiasm. The scenes are labeled with minimal scene setup identified. Concepts and ideas are introduced, and in some cases exact character dialog/lines are supplied. In others, room for 'improv' on the part of any given character is denoted, similar to the improv-comedy utilized in the production of Curb Your Enthusiasm.

Each episode outline begins with a cover page identifying the episode title, a short synopsis of the episode and the cast, including special guests. Each outline scene leads off with an identifier. For example:

1. EXT. LARRY IN HIS CAR, DRIVING INTO DOCTORS OFFICE BUILDING PARKING LOT – DAY (ONE)

This denotes Scene #1 is an exterior (EXT) scene, on day number ONE of the episode. The named character (**Larry**) is driving in his car and the setting for the scene is the parking lot of an office building.

Occasionally, there is a need for a character to pause during a dialog line (as if thinking before speaking). For this purpose, a series of periods (**...**) is used to denote the pause – e.g.: **Leon**: "You know, a pussy pad...and maybe even buy me a shagging wagon..."

Scene to scene transitions rely on the ability of the reader (viewer) to grasp and visualize the change in settings. For example, if a scene ends with the characters leaving an interior (INT) setting and the next scene is an exterior (EXT) shot, it's presumed that the characters walked outside. We chose to include explicit scene transition notes when there was a particularly complex scene change denoted by the identifier:

< SCENE TRANSITION >

Unless otherwise noted, scenes end with a 'fade out to black' and begin with a 'fade in from black'.

And finally, each episode has a theme or 'hook' which is the main thrust of the episode while one or more subplots are inserted to add some comic diversions.

Read! Enjoy! Laugh...out loud!
(Or, as Larry David wouldn't say...LOL.)

EXODUS – And they Fled...

The LOST Episodes - Curb Your Enthusiasm-Volume 2 is the second in our series. **The LOST Episodes-Volume 1** was *The Beginning* - GENESIS (summarized below). Volume 2 continues the concept, with EXODUS. In Volume 2, enjoy ten new outrageous, offensive, sidesplitting episodes and follow Ray and John's arc of success. Find out how Ray and John's material brought them to Hollywood. Read how it brought them onto the set of Curb Your Enthusiasm, including guest roles in the final episode of the ninth season. And discover what's in store for them and the future of Curb Your Enthusiasm.

The LOST Episodes - Curb Your Enthusiasm - Volume 1: The book of GENESIS: In the Beginning... there was darkness. The World's WORST Boss created a world (a project in LA) for us and appointed us as his regent. We proved disobedient and the World's WORST Boss tried to destroy us and our world (project) with his presumed POWER: flood(ing) us with threatening email and text messages. We weren't destroyed. Each and every success on our part only served to further infuriate the World's WORST Boss, which further motivated us and provided even more creative material.

The LOST Episodes - Curb Your Enthusiasm – Volume 2: The book of EXODUS: ...And they Fled. The World's Worst Boss practiced EVIL: 'my enemies, and my oppressors come near me to devour my flesh, they stumble and fall.'* Maybe not literally on the 'devour my flesh' part, but stumble and fall, they did. FIRED. We FLED. We ran from Evil and never...well... occasionally, looked back. We had to. The circumstance(s) we escaped from was a slow-motion-larger-than-life train-wreck. Eventually, Karma stepped in and righted a few wrongs.

Volume 2 of The LOST Episodes started out as a narrative of the downfall of all the flunkies that tormented us (John and Ray) while simultaneously documenting the rise and success of John and Ray and their writing. Success (and Ray's constant battle cry, "Envision IT") compelled us to abandon the negative material of the past and focus on the positive, current successes: John and Ray FLED. They DO escape the 'desert' and make it to the ~~Red~~ BLUE Sea (the Pacific Ocean/Hollywood).

* That bit about 'oppressors stumble and fall' isn't from Exodus, it's from Psalms. Just testing the hardcore believers.

If you read (or reread!) the episode chapters of this book after watching Season 9 of Curb Your Enthusiasm, you'll recognize some obvious parallels that appear in the actual Season 9 Episodes. Obviously we can't spill outright spoilers, but we can drop a few hints.

If you watch the (TV) episodes of Curb Your Enthusiasm closely, you'll notice snippets of scenes from this book (and Volume 1) have found their way into various episodes in Season 9. From irrationally behaved restaurant staff (Chapter 7/Episode 3-Guys & Dolls, scene 5) to Larry's donning of a disguise (going back to Volume 1 of The LOST Episodes–Chapter 10, the episode entitled, "Cluck YOU!"), to the apparent reconciliation of Larry and Cheryl (Chapter 5/Episode 2–Mirror, Mirror), the situations and dialog will be recognizable.

We experienced so much so fast. Being allowed onto the closed set of Curb Your Enthusiasm gave us experience that can't be learned from a book or taught in a class. For instance, the change from a 2-camera shoot to 3-camera significantly changed the documentary 'feel' of the show, or the repeated shooting of scenes to capture the best 'improv' lines, and even the shooting out-of-sequence and editing of episodes together to maintain continuity – all of this influenced how we wrote the episodes in this volume (and future episodes).

The last episode in this volume – Chapter 21/Episode 10 – '(Almost) No Place Like Home' has significant irony to us. Much like the lead character does in that episode, we unintentionally embarked on a long, exciting journey. We met a cast of interesting, upright people (and a few strange and evil characters) and eventually found our way to OZ (Los Angeles and Curb Your Enthusiasm). Over and over, Ray kept saying to John, "Envision IT". All that's left to envision is Larry David approving production of Curb Your Enthusiasm – Season 10. With multiple seasons worth of outrageous, offensive material already written and a database of THOUSANDS of comical ideas, our future is brighter with a Season 10 than without.

Worth a THOUSAND Words

For us (John and Ray), writing is the easy part. And, it's the BEST part. We can crank out ideas and scenarios by the dozens in a single afternoon. Need a thousand words by tomorrow? DONE!...where should we go for dinner tonight? The hard part—the drudgery that isn't always fun, is promoting our work.

We had been invited to a party in West Hollywood. It wasn't business related, but we also knew we weren't going to make new contacts sitting on our tails at the Manhattan Beach Starbucks...so we went. Ray called it before we even parked the car: 'Creep Show'. John looked towards the building where the party was being held and saw two women entering the party location and acknowledged: 'Elvira...twins'. This wasn't a costume party and nowhere near Halloween. Yet, here were two women, in public, together, both dressed to mimic Elvira, Mistress of the Dark (the cult-movie/TV character created by Cassandra Peterson).

> **John**: "Stay or leave?"
>
> **Ray**: "We have to stay. Maybe we score a double date with the Elvira twins? Envision IT!"
>
> **John**: "Sure...and maybe they drug us, dress us both up like Pee-wee Herman, handcuff all 4 of us to the front of Sony Studios, and we end up on Entertainment Tonight."
>
> **Ray**: "Pee-wee Herman? WHAT THE FUCK are you talking about?"

It was a 'stretch'. Cassandra Peterson (a.k.a., Elvira) had a cameo in the movie Pee-wee's Big Adventure.

We 'Envisioned IT' and went in. The place was the definition of creepy. The host had decorated his upscale loft with some unusual 'art'. Large framed hologram pictures— the type that have a green tint and a 3-d aspect to them, lined the walls. But these weren't everyday 3-d images—no soaring eagles or wolves leaping out. Not even dogs playing poker. All the 3-d holograms were porn. Hardcore porn. Raising the CREEP level one extra notch (if that were possible), the images appeared to shift positions as we walked past them. No matter where we stood—the body parts were always pointing right at us. We didn't touch anything. We certainly didn't eat or drink anything. We did, however, collect a ton of new material/ideas.

If in fact a picture is worth a thousand words, we had stumbled across an idea for FIVE thousand...

Episode 1

"Picture THIS!"

Synopsis: Larry's chance run-in with a disgraced celebrity at a movie theater gives Larry the opportunity to save the day during a birthday party at the Greene's house when the entertainment for the party cancels last minute.

Scenes: 15

Cast: Larry, Jeff, Susie, Sammi, Larry's girlfriend Greta, movie theater employee, artist family members, tribal chief.

Special Guest: Paul Reubens (as Paul Reubens & Pee-wee Herman).

"Picture THIS!"

1. INT. LARRY'S HOUSE - DAY (ONE)

LARRY is talking on the phone with his girlfriend, **GRETA**, making plans for the day. After debating with Greta and getting unsolicited input from Leon, Larry suggests they go to an 'Art House' movie since the crowds are always small. Larry leafs through a newspaper and picks a movie based on its length, (dismissing objections by Greta). The film has an erotic title and Greta questions Larry's motives. Greta (reluctantly) agrees to the selection. Larry mentions some errands he needs to do and will pick up Greta on the way to the art house theater. (Call ends.)

2. EXT./INT. LARRY'S CAR/JEFF'S HOUSE - DAY (ONE)

(SPLIT SCREEN) Larry is in his car, on the phone with **JEFF**. (Jeff is at his home office desk). Jeff has a painting on his desk (facing away from camera). Jeff tells Larry he just came home from an art auction where he bought an INCREDIBLE painting of 'this woman'.

Jeff: "It's so real, it's LIFELIKE...like you want to just TOUCH her (Jeff reaches out towards the painting). And it's a great investment...this hermit artist died suddenly last year, and you know how it is---as soon as an artist dies off, his works start to run up in value. You have to see it Larry...wherever you move in the room...it's like...she has these seductive eyes that follow you...I'm not kidding. I kinda get turned on every time I look at her...ahhh...it...I don't think I can leave this room...she wants ME, Larry, she wants ME."

Larry: "The picture wants you?...Does Susie know?"

Jeff: "I'm telling you Larry, the picture wants me!...It's hypnotic...like she has a spell or something on me."

Larry: "SPELL, SCHMELL. You don't believe in that spell bullshit...next thing you'll tell me is that you want to see a psychic card reader...or call Dionne Warwick, or some other shmutzik."

Jeff dismisses Larry's abrasive suggestions ('whatever') and asks Larry if he wants to go golfing, as he has no plans. Jeff suggests Larry could stop by to pick him up and see the painting. Larry tells Jeff he's 'trapped' into going to a movie with his girlfriend and can't get out of it. Jeff sympathizes and mentions to Larry that Sammi's birthday is this coming weekend and Susie has hired Sammi's favorite hip-hop DJ as a surprise to entertain Sammi and her friends. Jeff tells Larry he can't stand the music, but he knows Sammi will freak out when she sees the surprise DJ. Larry remarks about the good old days of hiring a pony or a clown.

Jeff: "Ponies and Clowns? Larry, that sort of thing is only done in porn now."

Larry: "Porn? Ponies and Clowns?..."

Larry (sarcastically) tells Jeff he will cancel the order for the pony and asks Jeff what he should get for Sammi since she's at such a transitional age. Larry offers few bizarre ideas to Jeff. Larry hates the idea of getting a simple gift card.

Jeff: "Be creative. BE CREATIVE. Put some thought into it."

Larry agrees. (Call ends.)

3. EXT. FRONT OF ART HOUSE MOVIE THEATER - DAY (ONE)

Larry approaches the ticket window with his girlfriend, Greta. The **TICKET AGENT** asks if he wants main floor tickets or balcony seats. Larry is confused.

Larry: "What's the difference? Is there a different cost or are there reserved seats?"

Ticket Agent (blinks his eyes several times, pauses 3-4 seconds and replies): "No difference."

Larry tries to clarify why ticket seller would ask. Greta pushes Larry to buy tickets and go. Walking towards the theatre entrance, Larry is still complaining about the absurd ticket options.

< SCENE TRANSITION >

As they pass the concession counter, Greta asks Larry to get popcorn. Larry looks at menu board -- there are 9 popcorn size choices. Larry rolls his eyes and groans. Larry asks the counter worker (facing away from Larry): 'Can I just get a large bucket?' The counter help turns (the same person as Ticket Seller, dressed differently) and replies with options/questions for popcorn choices (yellow corn or white corn, salt, low salt, no salt, spicy salt, real butter, organic butter, cheesy butter, free range butter, etc.).

Larry (does a double-take look at counter help, looks back towards ticket booth, and turns to Greta): "See what you've started?"

4. INT. INSIDE MOVIE THEATER - DAY (ONE)

Larry and Greta survey the theater – it's completely empty. Larry (holding the bucket of popcorn) says (sarcastically) to Greta (holding up the tickets): "THESE must be the 'RESERVED' seats". After several seat 'tests', Larry picks out seats and they settle in. Waiting for the film to start, Larry mentions to Greta that Jeff and Susie are throwing a birthday party for their daughter Sammi and they are getting her a hip-hop DJ. Larry asks Greta if she has any ideas for a gift for Sammi. Greta asks Larry what kind of girl is she. Larry comments on how she's becoming more and more like her mother each day and postpones the conversation until movie is over. (Theatre darkens).

Larry (whispers): "Let me ask you something...as long as theater is empty...when's the last time you 'fooled around' in a theater?"

Greta responds by 'seductively' placing her hand in Larry's lap and smiles at Larry. (The film starts). Larry and Greta begin to make-out. (Off-camera noise/candy wrapper tearing open is heard.) Larry and Greta pull back/interrupt the make-out session. Another customer (**PAUL REUBENS**—face not seen) takes a seat directly behind them. Larry's girlfriend quickly pulls her hand out of Larry's lap and sits up straight. The other customer loudly/ distractingly places a trench-coat over the seatback next to Larry. Larry looks at coat, then at customer, then back at coat then back at customer and then does 'double-take' look at customer. Paul Reubens (face now seen) character takes the coat back and puts it on his lap as Larry turns around to look again. Paul Reubens character offers Larry some popcorn from his bucket (Paul Reubens does a brief Pee-wee Herman laugh). Larry doesn't acknowledge the offer. (Rustling noises are heard). The trench-coat appears to be moving. Larry turns around and double-takes again—he turns back to Greta and nudges her, telling her: "Look". Greta refuses. (More rustling noises/movement from the trench-coat are seen/heard.)

Larry (to Greta): "Look. It's him. I'm telling you...IT'S HIM."

Paul Reubens 'SHUSHES' Larry and sprays spit with his 'sshhh'.

Larry is startled, grabbing/wiping his neck, and yelling.

Larry: "WHAT WAS THAT? (turning towards Paul Reubens.) Say it!! Don't SPRAY it. For Chrissakes!"

Paul Reubens (Pee-wee Herman voice): "Funny."

Larry (turns and whispers at Paul Reubens): "Let me ask you something. Did you ask for balcony or main floor tickets?"

Greta pokes Larry in the arm and says (in a stern tone): "Turn around!...Watch the movie!!". A few seconds later, a rustling/rubbing noise is heard from behind Larry. Larry tries not to turn around. Larry eventually turns to see what the disturbance/noise is behind him but sees nothing and turns back to the screen. A few seconds later, the noise is heard again. Larry turns quickly trying to catch Paul Reubens 'touching' himself but sees nothing and turns back to the screen. (Repeat several times). Greta gets upset at the constant commotion and yells at both of them.

Greta: "The BOTH OF YOU's. Shut Up, already!"

A theatre attendant (the same person as ticket/concessions worker, dressed differently) approaches. The attendant shines a flashlight at Larry's face, at Paul Reubens face, at the trench-coat in his lap and then at bucket of popcorn in Larry's lap. The attendant tells Larry and Paul the theater doesn't allow that sort of behavior and they have to leave. Larry and Paul Reubens argue and dispute the 'behavior' and claim it was the others 'fault'. Larry complains about the rustling/ruffling/rubbing noises.

Larry (to attendant): "Who comes into a theater alone with trench-coat?"

Larry suggests the attendant to look closer at Paul Reubens. The attendant declines and repeats they must leave. Paul Reubens tells the attendant that Larry was rude, disruptive, insulting and hurtful. Larry stands up and tells Greta: "Come on. We're leaving", while continuing to trade comments/insults with Paul Reubens.

Greta declines. She tells Larry she's staying to watch the film. Larry and Paul Reubens leave. Outside the theatre Larry and Paul Reubens continue the exchange of accusations/insults. Larry turns as if to leave, stops and looks at Paul Reubens.

Larry: "Let me ask you something…"

Paul Reubens (interrupts): "About 'THAT' night and what really happened?"

Paul Reubens tells Larry he was totally humiliated that night...he was having a severe reaction/rash to fabric softener that was on his underwear. Paul Reubens tells him he was 'Scratching'...NOT 'Jerking'. Larry gives him the 'Lie-Eye-Stare' and says, "Okay, I believe you". Paul Reubens goes on to tell how his life and career were ruined...destroyed...all because of fabric softener. Paul Reubens tells Larry that he has limited opportunities and he doesn't earn anywhere near what he once did and he may file for bankruptcy if work doesn't pick up. Paul Reubens asks Larry if he can help him out and how he would appreciate ANY type of work Larry could send his way.

Paul Reubens (handing Larry his business card): "Call me if 'ANYTHING' ...you know...POPS-UP!"

Larry: "Pops-up???"

Paul Reubens (does the Pee-wee Herman 'laugh'): "Anything, Larry."

Paul Reubens hands Larry his bucket of popcorn. Larry holds Paul Reubens' popcorn bucket above his head and looks at the bottom. Paul Reubens thanks Larry and leaves. Greta comes out of theatre (looks angry). She sees Larry and walks past him.

Greta: (Loudly) "GOOD-BYE!"...(quietly) "Asshole."

Larry (holds out the bucket): "Popcorn?...It's LIGHTLY buttered...No good?"

5. INT. JEFF'S HOUSE - DAY (TWO)

SUSIE and Jeff are in their home office. Susie is standing over Jeff (sitting at his desk) scowling at the painting (facing away from camera). Susie is RIPPING Jeff for bringing SMUT into HER house and tells Jeff she can't stand looking at it. Jeff argues. It's an art-investment—it's already 'collectible' as several other versions were destroyed by the model. Susie doesn't relent. She tells Jeff she doesn't want to see it. If he insists on keeping it, he can hang it in the attic or the back of a closet/somewhere out of the way. Susie steps back and looks at the picture.

Susie (to the painting): "What THE Fuck are YOU looking at?"

Susie (leaving Jeff's office/yells at Jeff): "Hang HER somewhere else.... OR I'LL HANG YOU SOMEWHERE ELSE."

Jeff: "Alright...alright...I'll find a place for it."

Jeff looks at the picture and smiles.

Jeff (to the picture): "Pay no attention to that mean lady...she's just the cleaning woman...it'll just be us together later tonight."

6. INT. RESTAURANT - DAY (THREE)

Larry & Jeff are seated at a table in a restaurant. They are discussing Sammi's upcoming birthday party and Larry is still without a gift idea. Jeff talks about the art painting and how he feels almost like he's cheating on Susie with her (the painting).

Jeff: "Two or three times a day I 'visit' the picture..."

Larry: "Visit?"

Jeff (ashamed) admits he jerked off to it twice the previous day.

Larry: "A painting? Why can't you just download porn like everyone else? A painting???"

Jeff says it's like having a new girlfriend.

Jeff: "Once you look into those sexy eyes you're done, Larry (Jeff makes a jerking off motion)...kinda like...who was that statue... Medusa?...you look into those eyes, and you're DONE!"

Larry: "Medusa???"

Larry asks Jeff where he's put the picture. Jeff says he's decided he's not going to hang the picture...he's going to keep it mobile–the way galleries do it. He will move it from room to room.

Larry (considers the concept for a moment): "A mobile painting...I LIKE it. No holes in walls, no hooks, no wires and it changes the atmosphere from room to room...never the same old room décor again."

Jeff: "Exactly."

Jeff tells Larry that he leans the picture against the wall in any room he likes. Larry asks where the picture is now? ("which room?"). Jeff says he tries to keep it one room 'ahead' of Susie...so that they are never in the same room together.

Jeff: "It's in the main-floor powder room...she only uses that once a month."

Larry (patronizing Jeff) asks if he's going to 'christen' each room in the house with one of his 'trysts' with the painting. Jeff (defensive) tells Larry he should stop by the house and see for himself.

Jeff: "Experience the art before you judge it."

Larry says he will. Jeff reminds Larry that Susie really dislikes the painting not to say anything to her about it if he stops by.

7. INT. LARRY'S HOUSE - DAY (THREE)
Larry is talking to Leon about Sammi's party and that Susie and Jeff hired a DJ. Leon asks what kind of DJ? ("because there's a difference").

Larry: "What difference?...you put on a few CDs, play a few songs and the girls jump around."

Leon tells Larry there's a vibe that goes with it.
Leon stands up to show Larry the difference. Leon demonstrates what he refers to as a few 'white person Barry Manilow' dance moves and then shows Larry some 'true Hip Hop moves' (with sexual overtones). Leon asks Larry to 'experience the difference'. Larry tries a few moves but doesn't have any rhythm.

Leon: "Larry, sit the fuck down and never do that again."

Larry asks Leon for gift ideas for Sammi. Leon offers a few 'inappropriate' ideas (a case of Malt Liquor, a pack of condoms, does she do X?). Larry dismisses the suggestions and tells Leon about running into Paul Reubens at the movie theatre the previous night. Leon makes a comment about Pee-wee jerking off in the theatre and how he would do the same thing. Leon talks about the 'pig-in-a-blanket' stunt.

Larry: "I don't know that one? Is it like the 'popcorn bucket-hole-in-the-bottom' trick?"

Leon: "The pig-in-a-blanket...you buy a hotdog and throw away the dog but keep the bun...you see what I'm sayin'?"

Larry: "So you waste a perfectly good hotdog just to use the bun? That's idiotic!"

Leon asks Larry to explain the 'popcorn bucket-hole' trick. Larry explains it.

Leon: "What kinda sick motherfucker would waste a whole bucket of popcorn and get his junk all greasy an' shit?...That's some SICK SHIT, LD."

Leon: "Whatever happened to your movie date the other night? Did you 'bring it' Larry? The best ass is movie theatre ass."

Larry says he should have used the popcorn bucket trick but now it's too late and "I didn't like her attitude". Leon comments that Larry needs to tap more ass and bring the bitches to the crib, but he needs to spice up the house with color and sexy mood shit. Leon tells Larry he needs to get some fluffy pillows, feathers and something to look at besides the TV and 1960s wallpaper. Larry looks around at his décor and nods in agreement. Larry: "…maybe some art pieces." Larry tells Leon about Jeff's investment painting. Larry describes the painting to Leon and tells him Jeff claims the model is so hot, she's hypnotic - that Jeff can't look at her without getting horny.

Leon: "Horny? Some naked bitch on a painting? That ain't horny, that's whipped, like pussy whipped."

Larry: "Yeah…you could say pussy whipped."

Larry tells Leon they should go see it and 'experience' whatever the hell Jeff is talking about. Leon agrees.

Leon: "Let's go see this hypno-pussy."

8. EXT./INT JEFF'S HOUSE/FRONT DOOR - DAY/NIGHT (THREE)

Larry and Leon ring the bell at the front door of Jeff's house. Jeff answers the door, invites them in and tells them says that Susie is out shopping for Sammi's party and won't be back for a while. Jeff invites Larry and Leon to sit. Jeff's cell phone rings. Susie is calling to ask Jeff questions about the party (colors for plates, napkins, balloons, etc.). While Jeff continues the phone conversation with Susie, Larry stands and whispers to Jeff, "bathroom" and leaves. Jeff ends the phone call. The powder (bath) room door opens and Larry stumbles out–his shirt half un-tucked and hair a mess.

Larry: "WOW!"

Jeff: "You saw it? Hypnotic, Right? Hottest chick EVER, RIGHT?"

Larry talks of wanting get the same type of painting for his house.

Jeff: "It's an original...a one of a kind, and the artist is dead."

Larry continues to rave about the painting.

Leon: "It's only a painting. You two must be hard up for some real pussy if two grown men can't handle a picture of some fine ass bitch! That's some fucked up shit right there."

Leon stands up.

Larry: "Don't go in there...you'll turn to stone."

Jeff: "Or WOOD, at least."

Leon walks toward the powder room.

Larry (calls after him): "DON'T look into her eyes..."

Leon (walking towards the bathroom) talking to himself: "Bitch ain't never had THE Black man...get ready...daddy gonna teach you some lessons."

(Camera close-up on wall clock; Minute and second hands spinning fast: 5 minutes, 10 minutes, 20 minutes.)

Larry (shouting): "What's going on in there?"

(No response from Leon.)

Larry: "LEON!...put it away already."

Larry looks at Jeff.

Jeff: "See...hypnotic. I told you."

The bathroom door opens slowly and Leon comes out 'strutting' and zipping up his fly. Leon walks towards Jeff and sits on couch. Jeff asks Larry to come with him into the kitchen. Jeff asks Larry to sample a batch of cookies (burnt-black) Susie just made for Sammi's party.

Larry: "mmmm, no thanks...kinda full...and not a real big fan of Susie's cooking experiments."

Jeff realizes he forgot to buy candles for the cake and asks Larry to buy some and bring them for the party. Larry and Jeff re-enter the living room and Leon is sound asleep on the couch (mouth open, drool and snoring).

Jeff: "See. She GOT him."

Larry: "The painting?"

Jeff: "The painting."

Larry (nodding): "The painting."

9. EXT. LARRY'S CAR - DAY/NIGHT (THREE)
Larry and Leon are in the Prius driving down a street. Larry tells Leon he needs to stop at a store to buy some candles for Sammi's cake. Larry groans about the variety of candles.

Larry: "tall, short, fat, multi-colored, and those damn things you can't blow out. I really hate those goddamn candles. You pull them out of the cake thinking they are out, but when you touched them, they re-light and burn your fingers and some spill wax all over the cake."

Larry realizes he's not getting a response from Leon and turns to look at Leon who is sound asleep.

Larry (shaking his head): "You poor bastard. You must have looked DEEP into her eyes and that painting made you its bitch…"

Larry stops the car in front of a candle store.

10. INT. LARRY'S HOUSE - DAY (FOUR)

Larry is in his home office, talking on the phone with Jeff. Jeff asks about the candles ('Susie has been driving me NUTS with every little detail'). Larry assures him - he stopped off on the way home and bought two boxes, just in case some are defective. Larry tells Jeff that he couldn't come up with a gift for Sammi and will get her a gift card. Jeff asks Larry to hold, Susie is calling him again and she'll hang his balls up as party decorations if he doesn't' answer. Jeff returns to call with Larry (sounds anxious/ panicked). Jeff tells Larry that Susie just gave him some bad news about Sammi's party and Susie's having a total meltdown. The DJ Susie hired for Sammi's party just cancelled and she just told Jeff to 'FIX IT'. Larry asks what happened and Jeff tells him the DJ's parole was revoked and he's back in jail. Larry suggests, as a birthday gift to Sammi, he could bail/bond out the DJ. Jeff fears Susie going 'nuclear' if he doesn't do something quickly. Jeff tells Larry she's really pissed off.

Jeff: "You know how she can get when she's pissed off... I'll be lucky to sleep in the garage."

Larry agrees. Larry picks up the Paul Reubens' business card from his desk and stares at it momentarily and tells Jeff he will take care of EVERYTHING.

Larry: "Tell Susie not to worry, I've got it covered."

Jeff: "Covered? Covered How? Are you going to get me into one of those Witness Protection Programs?"

Larry won't tell Jeff his (brilliant) idea. He assures Jeff he can take care of everything and will arrange for the entertainment --- a surprise 'gift' to be at Jeff's house for the start of the party. Jeff tells Larry that there's only two hours before the party...and if he doesn't come through, they'll both have to flee to the International Space Station...and THAT may not be far enough to hide from Susie.

11. INT. JEFFS HOUSE - DAY (FOUR)

(Wide shot of Jeff's front door, from the inside). The doorbell rings. Jeff and Susie approach and open the door. Larry is standing in the doorway alone, with an arm stretched to one side. Larry 'pulls' his surprise into the doorway opening: Paul Reubens, dressed as Pee-wee Herman. (Larry raises/opens his arms to show off his surprise gift and his ability to 'come through'). Jeff and Susie stand speechless/in shock. Larry introduces Susie and Jeff to their entertainment for the afternoon. Susie grabs Larry's arm and pulls him aside to have a discussion. Susie (quietly, but angry) tells Larry he really fucked up Sammi's party. While Susie is ripping Larry, Sammi and her friends walk in and see Paul Reubens/Pee-wee standing in the doorway. Sammi asks if this is the 'big surprise' Jeff and Susie were planning (Sammi and her friends' crowd around Pee-wee). Pee-wee makes some remarks and entertains them with his humor. Sammi and her friends are thrilled and pull Pee-wee into the decorated birthday room. Susie tries to stop Sammi but Paul Reubens is surrounded by the group and entertaining them with the Pee-wee character. Susie tells Jeff to do something. Jeff shrugs/raises his hands in the air. Susie turns to Larry and reprimands him for bringing a 'pervert' to their daughter's birthday party.

Susie: "You just couldn't think of a different gift, could you, you pathetic fuck!? I don't want my daughter EXPOSED to that (Susie makes a jerking-off motion). I swear, if he so much as scratches himself in front of her, Larry..."

Larry tells Susie not to worry. Sammi and her friends are not old enough to remember Pee-wee/Paul Reubens was involved in that 'incident'.

Susie: "You better hope so...or you're going to have to see a proctologist to get THESE back." (Susie grabs the two boxes of birthday candles from Larry's hand.)

(A scream is heard off camera). Larry, Jeff and Susie run towards the sound of the scream (the powder room). A girl comes out of the bathroom looking flustered/disoriented.

Jeff (looks at Larry and mouths): "The painting."

Larry nods. Susie takes the girl to the kitchen to find out

what happened and comfort her. Larry says he needs to use the bathroom. Jeff blocks the door.

Jeff: "BROKEN. Use the upstairs bathroom!"

Larry argues that it isn't broken and why should he go all the way upstairs?

Jeff: "Just go!...You know why!"

Susie (yelling for Jeff): "Jeffrey...honey...Please come in here...NOW!!!!"

Jeff (mouths): "Fuck!"

Jeff gestures to Larry to go upstairs and walks towards the kitchen. Larry pauses on stairs, looks back, turns around and walks to the 1st floor powder/bath room. Larry pauses, 'fixes' his hair and checks his breath before entering the bathroom.

12. EXT. REMOTE ISLAND BEACHFRONT - NIGHT (FOUR)

A night-time ceremony of undetermined ritual is taking place. Several 'normal' dressed people are standing next to a group dressed in tribal costumes. All are gathered around a bonfire. There is chanting, fire flare-ups, dancing, drums, etc. Framed paintings are being thrown into the fire. (Subtitles translate the chants). The subtitles indicate the tribal ceremony is an appeal to the remove the curse that lives on through paintings the artist created before his recent death. The fire grows larger and more intense. The subtitles translate to indicate the (dead) artist is disturbed and angry. The group appears scared and say they doubt the ceremony will break the curse.

Tribal Chief (subtitled): "The curse will continue unbroken. He who looks into the painting will fall under the spell and will be driven to terrible acts of…impurity."

13. INT. JEFF'S HOUSE – NIGHT (FOUR)
Larry appears to be in a trance, walking through Jeff's living room. He stares blankly, eyes wide open, a faint smirk on his face. Susie sees Larry.

Susie: "What the fuck, Larry…are you stoned?"
Larry snaps out of the trance and seems confused/ disoriented.

Susie: "I swear Larry…if you're going to have a stroke, go do it at home. I don't want you spoiling Sammi's party by dying here."

Loud music/talking/laughter is heard in background.

< SCENE TRANSITION - to party room >

Sammi's friends are telling Sammi how great the party was and how they all want Pee-wee Herman for their birthday party! Unnamed friend to Sammi: 'You're lucky to have such great parents!' Sammi is pleased by her friend's reaction and smiles at Jeff and Susie. Susie and Jeff look at each other in astonishment, then to Larry to give him a 'good job' nod of approval. Larry pats himself on the back. Sammi approaches Susie and Jeff and thanks them for their surprise gift --- she would never have guessed she would have the cutest, coolest and funniest entertainer for her special day. (Sammi hugs Jeff and Susie.)

Jeff: "You should give Larry a big thank you since he helped too."

Sammi hesitates, awkwardly gives Larry a hug and says 'thank you, Larry'. Susie tells Larry and Jeff she's going to go apologize to Pee-wee for her attitude and the way she behaved when he arrived. Susie tells Jeff he should give Paul Reubens a nice fat tip before he leaves.
Jeff agrees. Susie walks away to look for Pee-wee.

Jeff (to Larry): "I never thought you could pull something like this off!"

Larry shrugs/gestures/gives a humorous/smug look.

Jeff: "You don't know how happy this made Susie...and more importantly, you saved my balls."

Jeff motions to give Larry a hug...Larry pushes back and refuses.

Larry: "Keep your balls to yourself."

Susie returns saying she can't find Pee-wee and tells Jeff and Larry to find him.

14. INT. JEFF'S HOUSE – NIGHT (FOUR)
Jeff's home office (the room is empty and poorly lit). (Camera-shot close-up on Jeff's office answering machine. The answering machine indicates 16 missed calls and 15 messages.) The phone rings, the answering machine picks up and an audible message is left.

Unknown Caller (audio dub: 'creepy' voice with accent): "Mr. Greene...we've been trying to reach you regarding the painting you purchased. It's imperative that you contact us, immediately. It's possible...there may be...that is...we believe something is terribly wrong...it's possible you or your family may be in danger. There have been some unusual occurrences that befell the purchasers of this artist's other paintings. It all sounds rather absurd, but the surviving members of the artist's family have presented evidence that the artist practiced some unusual ...shall we say, religious habits and we are told his paintings carry a...ahhh, well, the words the family used were 'curse' and 'hypnotic powers'...and given the most peculiar behaviors exhibited by the other purchasers, the family is requesting return of the painting immediately. You will, of course, receive a full refund plus we are prepared to cover all your expenses. Please contact us directly and we will send a courier over at once with your refund and pick up the picture...again...please contact us immediately as you may be in danger."

15. INT. JEFF'S HOUSE - NIGHT(FOUR)

Larry is walking through the house, casually looking for Pee-wee and hears a faint rustling/rubbing/scratching noise. Susie and Jeff approach Larry. Susie asks Larry if he's seen Pee-wee. Larry says no, and asks Susie and Jeff if they hear the rustling/rubbing/scratching noise. Susie hears it.

Susie: "What the hell's that?"

Jeff: "Where's it coming from?"

Larry, Susie and Jeff all turn to survey the room, trying to determine where the sound is coming from. Larry, Susie and Jeff move toward the hallway and Larry says it's coming from inside the bathroom. Larry then notices/points out that Pee-wee's suitcoat is caught in the closed bathroom door latch. Susie knocks on bathroom door.

Susie: "Pee-wee?...Paul...Whatever your name is...Is everything okay?"

(No response. The rustling/scratching noise continues.)

Susie pounds on the bathroom door and it pops opens. Larry, Jeff and Susie are all looking into the bathroom (side shot from camera) with horrified/shocked looks on their faces.

(Paul Reubens does the Pee-wee Herman 'laugh').

FADE OUT/Cue Music.

(END)

- 4 -

HAPPY Endings!

There were both good and bad moments as our adventure into screen and book writing progressed. Moments when we were sure that God hated us. But then some rays of light would appear. Ray would yell, "ENVISION IT". John would say, "SCREW IT, We'll make our own luck". And life was good again.

Volume 1 of The LOST Episodes was doing well. It was (is) on Amazon.com and Barnes & Noble picked it up. We were getting top-rated reviews and at one point, Volume 1 reached #6 in sales in the Amazon humor section. Karma had turned our way. Fans had demanded more, so we embarked on The LOST Episodes - Volume 2. While that was in progress, we began getting interest in our work and inquiries from production companies/small studios. One wanted to turn Volume 1 of The LOST Episodes into a comic-animation series. Another wanted us to 're-tune' the episodes for a different (generic) sitcom. We had to make some tough choices. We were selling some of our standup (comedy) material and some of our ghost writing work was very well received (although of little significance, since we couldn't be credited for it), but our primary focus was towards Curb Your Enthusiasm. We wanted to stay true to our plan and it felt as if we were close to our ultimate goal of getting our material into the right hands.

We had been writing for nearly seven years, and if we had been cursed by bad people, bad timing or just plain bad luck, the curse had been lifted.

Good luck may come and go. Good Karma is the perpetual reflection in the...

Episode 2

"Mirror, Mirror"

Synopsis: Larry's fortunes take a turn for the better as the source of a long run of inexplicable bad luck is revealed, only to have history repeat itself.

Scenes: 14

Cast: Larry, Larry's girlfriend Norene, Cheryl, Jeff, Susie, Leon, Richard Lewis, Antoinette, Santa Anita Racetrack* Clerk, Police Woman, misc. restaurant staff, misc. women on street, Salon Pedicurists, Drive-Thru girl.

Special Guest: Lou Ferrigno

*Ray and John would spend an occasional afternoon at the now defunct Hollywood Park casino-racetrack—the original setting for the racetrack in Mirror, Mirror. It was a fantastic place to sit in the sun, meet interesting characters, and ignore moronic messages from the World's WORST Boss.

"Mirror, Mirror"

1. INT. LARRY IN BED AT HIS GIRLFRIENDS HOME – DAY (ONE)

LARRY is in bed with his girlfriend, **NORENE,** kissing her enthusiastically. He kisses her face, then neck, and works his way down her chest to her genital area. Norene is moaning. While Larry is 'going down' on Norene, he hears LOUD snoring. Larry calls out to Norene and gets no response. Larry tries to gently wake her and (still) gets no response. Larry shakes the bed (her head bouncing up and down) and still gets no response. Larry spots a bottle of prescription medication on the nightstand and looks at it/reads the label (out loud): "For Narcolepsy". The girlfriend continues snoring loudly. Larry can't believe the amount of noise coming out of her mouth. Larry hurries to get dressed while covering his ears. Larry turns to leave, pauses, pulls his phone from his pocket, taps the screen a few times, and quickly exits.

2. INT. JEFF'S OFFICE WITH LARRY - DAY (TWO)

Larry tells **JEFF** about his date and how she fell asleep while he was 'going down' on her. Jeff remarks about Larry losing his touch. Larry explains the medication he found next to her bed for narcolepsy. (Jeff laughs). Larry tells Jeff how he couldn't wake her up no matter how hard he tried and that she has the LOUDEST snore on the planet. Jeff disputes loudest snore.

Jeff: "The world snoring champion, according to Susie, is ME."

Larry tells Jeff that he recorded her incredibly loud snore because he knew nobody would believe him.

Jeff: "You secretly recorded it? Donald Trump will be tweeting about you."

Larry plays the sound clip back from his phone. He places the phone on desk and phone is 'jumping' around desk from vibration/noise. Jeff is amazed how loud it is and suggests it would be funny if Larry would make that into a 'ring-tone'. Larry likes the idea. Jeff shows Larry how to make it a ring-tone so every time someone calls, the loud snore ring-tone will sound. Larry is pleased with new ringtone. Larry notices gift cards on Jeff's desk and inquires about them. Jeff says he bought spa pedicures for the girls in the office for Admin Day but two were on vacation, so there are two cards left over. Jeff asks Larry if he's ever had a pedicure. Larry says no/he never liked the idea. Jeff convinces Larry how great it is to have someone rub your feet and legs, manicure your toes and how incredibly refreshing it is. Larry says he's not fond of strangers touching his feet but agrees to try it. Larry says he is very ticklish and probably won't be able to keep still. Jeff assures Larry that won't be a problem and he will setup the appointments. Larry looks at his watch and announces he needs to get home to watch a live horse race on television. Jeff (tries to) question Larry about the race, but Larry is already excusing himself/leaving the office.

3. INT. LARRY'S HOUSE - DAY (TWO)
Larry is sitting on his living room couch watching 'live' Horse Racing on the television, holding a Santa Anita Park OTB betting slip in his hand. **LEON** enters the room. Larry tells Leon that he received a 'hot' tip on the horse race and he placed a big bet. Leon asks Larry if he has ever made money playing the ponies. Larry says he used to do

alright, but for the longest time he has had bad luck. Larry is confident that THIS time is different since he has 'inside information'. The horse race begins. Larry is yelling at the television.

Larry: "Go!...Come On, FishLips!...Go!"

Leon: "Seriously, LD? FishLips? Ain't no pony named FishLips gonna be in the money."

Larry's horse jumps into the lead.

Larry: "He's winning. He's WINNING!"
(The horse loses ground.)

Larry: "He's losing. He's LOSING...Come On, FishLips!...Go!"
(The horse jumps back into the lead.)

Larry: "He's winning. He's WINNING!"

Larry's horse finishes dead last by 10 lengths. Larry is crushed. Leon tells Larry it looks like his luck still stinks. Larry picks up the phone and calls the person that gave him the 'tip'. The 'insider' makes excuses (audio dub) and can't understand why the horse lost – it was 'solid information', and gives Larry another tip for tomorrow's race ('it's a SURE THING') and assures Larry that he will make back his money from today's race and a lot more tomorrow...Guaranteed. The 'insider' tells Larry to bet big on the horse named 'Bob's Weary'. Larry agrees and says he will make a trip to the Santa Anita Park to place the bet. Larry asks Leon if he wants to go with him to Santa Anita tomorrow to place a bet then grab some lunch. Leon agrees.

4. INT. LARRY & JEFF AT NAIL SALON - DAY (THREE)

Larry and Jeff arrive at the nail salon for the pedicures. Jeff and Larry are the only men in the busy/full salon.

Jeff (to (Asian) girl at the counter): "We are here for our pedicure appointments...Greene and David!"

Counter girl (with heavy 'Asian' accent): "Mista Gleen and Mista Day-wid!"

Larry (smirking at the mispronunciation of their names): "Yes...Gleen and Day-wid."

Two **SALON GIRLS** (Asian - one young and cute and one older and expressionless) approach Jeff and Larry and introduce themselves (with heavy 'Asian' accents) as their pedicurists and ask them to follow. Larry and Jeff follow, quietly arguing who gets the young cute one. (Subtitles show the two Asian women discussing which one gets the fat guy and which one the old, bald guy). Jeff and Larry sit in the pedicure chairs and are asked to remove their shoes and socks and begin soaking their feet. The pedicurists leave and return – the 'young-cute' pedicurist goes to Jeff and the 'older expressionless' one goes to Larry. The 'young-cute' girl tells Larry that his pedicurist's name is Yashica and she speaks very little English, so she will be translating. Yashica is also the salon's owner, and an expert pedicurist. It is rare that she attends to a new customer and Larry should feel "Rucky!" Larry looks into the expressionless lady's eyes ('Lie-Eye-Stare') and says: "Okay".

As Jeff and Larry are soaking their feet, the Asian girls rub/massage their calves. Jeff and Larry are enjoying the treatment.

Larry (to Jeff): "Not...too...bad."

Jeff: "Did I tell you, Did I tell YOU? Best foot job in town."

The Asian girls are toweling off Jeff and Larry's feet and begin the foot massage. Jeff (moaning) tells Larry how much he likes having his feet rubbed (other customers staring). Larry watches Yashica (expressionless) put a handful of (pink) lotion on her hands and prepare to rub his feet. Jeff continues to relate how great the feeling is as his pedicurist is smiling and joking with Jeff. Larry tries to make small talk with his pedicurist but she does not acknowledge Larry. Larry returns to staring at Jeff and his pedicurist and is startled (body flinches) by the cold (pink colored) lotion as his pedicurist touches his feet to begin the foot massage. Larry reacts to the sensation (pulling back) and tells the pedicurist, ("kinda ticklish"). The pedicurist does not respond and continues rubbing. Larry flinches and then his foot/leg shoots straight out kicking his pedicurist in the face knocking her out.

Jeff: "What the fuck!"

Larry looks at his pedicurist on the floor and jumps out of his chair to see if she is ok (she remains unconscious).

Larry stares at her briefly and turns to Jeff.

Larry: "Is it me, or does it appear she has a smile on her face?"

Jeff: "You knocked her out!...What the fuck, Larry?"

Several (Asian) salon workers surround the knocked out pedicurist/owner (yelling/swearing in Mandarin and making hand gestures at Larry). The salon counter-girl approaches and yells at Larry: "Fatwa. Fatwa." Jeff tells Larry that they should leave immediately before they get jumped. Jeff and Larry run out without their shoes or socks. Jeff stops, yells at Larry that he needs his shoes. Larry is trying to wipe the large pink glob of cream off his foot. Larry replies that it's not wise to go back in there for their shoes and should go back when things settle down (camera shows them hobbling away/towards their cars, barefoot with their dress pants rolled up). Larry continues to wipe the pink lotion off his foot as he walks.

5. EXT. LARRY'S CAR - DAY (THREE)

Larry and Leon are driving to Santa Anita Park. Larry tells Leon about his pedicure adventure. While stopped at a traffic light, Leon checks out a hot girl crossing the street. Leon tries to get a response out of Larry on the girl's looks. Larry shows no interest. As the girl passes in front of Larry's Prius, Leon reaches over and 'honks' the car horn. The girl casually turns her head, looks at Larry, gives him a long stare, and eventually, a smile. Larry returns the smile. Leon tells Larry he needs to be more aggressive with the ladies if he plans on getting pussy. Leon tells Larry he better 'USE IT' before he 'LOSES IT' and he should be happy he can still get it up at his age. Larry and Leon argue over the age and performance comment. Larry's cell phone rings (caller ID shows its Antoinette). Antoinette reminds Larry of several appointments and that Admin Day is coming up. Larry thanks her and ends the call. Larry tells

Leon he's stopping at a drug store to pick up a box of chocolates for Antoinette for Admin Day.

6. INT. SANTA ANITA PARK BETTING FACILITY - DAY (THREE)

Larry and Leon walk into Santa Anita Park. Larry tells Leon he wants to get in and out of there quickly.

Larry: "I'm just going to place this bet and leave...no dilly dally."

Leon: "Who said anything about pussy?"

Leon tells Larry he is thirsty and is going to get a soda. Larry asks Leon to bring him back one. Leon asks what kind of soda Larry wants. Larry tells Leon: 'I'll have whatever you're having'. Leon asks Larry for money. Larry hesitates, gives Leon some money and tells him to 'make it quick'. Larry, standing in line to place his bet, is studying the racing program looking for the horse he was told to bet on. The line that Larry is standing in is moving extremely slow. Larry jumps to the adjoining line that was moving faster. The 'new' line becomes slow and the original line is now moving quickly. Larry tries to get back into his place in original line. The other betters in line call him on it: "Once you leave your spot in line, you start at the back of the line again!". Larry argues without success and goes to the back of the line. Leon arrives with two sodas and asks Larry why he is still in line. Leon asks Larry the name of the horse he plans to bet.

Larry: "The horse's name is Bob's Weary."

Leon: "Sounds like a tired ole donkey..."

Larry is looking at the racing form and the betting odds board. Waiting in line to bet, Leon asks to see the racing program. Leon picks out a horse and asks Larry if it looks any good.

Larry: "It looks GOOD... GOOD for the glue factory."

Leon asks Larry if he's going to bet his money based on info from the same guy that gave him the losing tip the previous day? Larry says, "Yes, it's a sure thing." Larry takes a sip of soda. Larry turns to Leon.

Larry: "Green River soda?"

Leon: "It's good, right?"

Larry says he has not had Green River since he was a kid and forgot how good it is.

Larry: "Where's the straw and lid?"

Leon: "They ran out of lids. Can't use a straw without a lid."

Larry: "Why can't you use a straw without a lid?"

Leon: "The lid has a hole...like a pussy. You stick the straw in the hole, like a dick!...No pussy!...No dick!"

Larry pauses to think about it and nods. Leon studies the racing program closely for a moment.

Leon: "Number 5, Wet Claver is gonna win."

Larry looks at the history and odds on Leon's pick and laughs.

Larry: "Not a chance!...what kind of name is Wet Claver? Might as well call that horse Glue Shart!"

Leon insists it will win and wants to bet on 'Wet Claver'. Leon asks Larry to 'borrow' him $50.00. Larry looks at Leon and asks him what happened to his money. Leon says he left his wallet at home. Larry (shaking his head) hands Leon $50.00. Larry and Leon place bets and walk away from the betting counter holding their Green River sodas and betting slips. Larry is talking to Leon when a beautiful girl catches his attention. She gives Larry a long stare and smiles. Larry and Leon (still walking) watch her walk by, turning their heads to look at her back side.

While looking backwards at the girl, Larry collides with **LOU FERRIGNO** (standing next to a table with a pile of books). Larry spills his Green River soda all over Lou Ferrigno's crisp white dress shirt.

Larry (staring at the green stain): "Oh my God! ...I'm so sorry!...HOLY SH..."

Larry realizes it's Lou Ferrigno. Larry alternates looking at Lou Ferrigno's face and white shirt stained with Green River soda.

Larry (to Leon): "Oh shit!...It's The Hulk."

Larry (to Lou): "Don't get angry Lou!...I...wouldn't like it...I'll make this right. I'll take care of your shirt."

Lou Ferrigno appears 'upset'. The books on the table are there for a promotion (poster behind Lou announces Lou is signing copies of his book, "*My Incredible Life As The Hulk*"). Lou looks at the books. The books on the table are splashed with Green River.

Lou (to Larry): "It would BEHOOVE you to leave...NOW!"

Larry (looking at Leon/quietly says): "Behoove?...what's that?"

Leon: "It means, let's get the fuck out of here before he behooves our asses! Offer to him that you'll buy ALL the books on the table!"

Larry (to Lou): "I'll tell you what Lou, it would be my pleasure to replace your shirt and as my sincere gesture of apology, I will buy ALL the books on the table."

Lou 'calms down' and agrees. Larry then picks up a copy and begins flipping through it. Larry's cell phone rings (LOUD SNORE RINGTONE) and Lou Ferrigno hears the 'snoring' noise. Lou thinks Larry is making the snoring noise while flipping through his book. Lou becomes 'angry' and tells Larry he will snap him in half if he does that again!

Larry: "Do what?"

Lou: "Make a snoring sound when looking at my book!"

Larry realizes it was his ringtone on his phone and tries to explain it to Lou but Lou is upset/not listening.

Leon (to Larry): "Pay the man and let's get the..."

< SCENE TRANSITION – PARKING LOT **>**

Leon and Larry exit Santa Anita Park each holding an armful of books.

Leon: "You did the right thing, LD...Lou would have fucked you up."

7. EXT. DRIVING PRIUS ON STREET– DAY (THREE)

Larry and Leon are in the car leaving the horse track. Leon is talking about the potential payoff if his horse wins. Leon tells Larry about all the 'wild shit' he's going do with the winnings. Larry talks about his plans with his winnings. They are debating their spending plans when Larry sees police-car (flashing) lights in his rear-view mirror.

Leon: "Did Lou call THE MAN on you? Pull over."

Larry pulls over to side of the road.

Leon: "I don't know anyone with as much bad luck as Larry David!"

A (black-female) **OFFICER** arrives at Larry's car window. Larry rolls window down and asks the officer what seems to be the problem. The officer tells Larry he was speeding. Larry disputes it. The officer tells Larry to stay in his car and she will be right back. Larry ignores the 'stay in the car' request and exits the car to talk to the officer. Leon looks at the box of chocolates Larry purchased for Antoinette. He opens the package and begins sampling them. Leon takes a bite out of one, makes a 'disgusted' face and puts the piece back in the box. He tries another, doesn't like that one, replaces it, and takes a third piece. (Camera transitions to Larry near police car). The officer tells Larry he was going 6 miles per hour over the speed limit.

Larry (argues): "That's not speeding...it's driving with a purpose!"

The officer becomes impatient with Larry and says she will cuff him and take him to the station if he wants to be difficult. She tells Larry get back in his car. (Larry returns to his car). Leon sees Larry is upset and tells Larry not to worry and he will 'handle it'. The officer approaches Larry's car window. Leon begins to flirt/joke with the female officer (makes her laugh). The officer hands Leon a card with her contact information on it and tells Leon if he would like to hang out with her to call her. Larry looks at Leon and is astonished at his smooth moves. Larry turns back towards the officer and she has her arm extended handing him a speeding ticket. Larry can't believe it and asks (out loud) "What else can possibly go wrong?". Leon tells Larry he's hungry and for Larry to "take it like a man and let's go get lunch". Larry replies he's going to go extra slow since he was just speeding a FULL SIX miles per hour over the limit.

8. EXT. LARRY'S CAR AT FAST FOOD DRIVE THROUGH WINDOW - DAY (THREE)

Larry and Leon at a fast food drive-up menu board placing their order. Larry places his order via the intercom-speaker. The **ORDER-TAKER** girl (Asian/seen thru pick up window) is confused and asks Larry to repeat (multiple times). The order taker asks Larry if he would like Flies (fries). Larry asks Leon what she means by 'flies'.

Order taker: "Drink?"

Larry asks if they have Green River.

Order-taker: "Gleen LIVER?"

Larry: "Oh forget it. Just give me a Coke."

Order-taker: "What SIGH? (size)."

Larry asks Leon what she means by 'SIGH'.

Larry: "ANY sigh – Large, extra Large, GIVE me a bucket full."

Leon places his order. Leon flirts with order-taker and makes her laugh. Larry pulls up to the window to pay and pick up their food. Leon smiles at the drive-thru girl and tells Larry to 'tip' her. Larry says you don't tip drive-thru people..."It's just not done!" Leon presses Larry to tip 'a few bucks' and see what happens. Larry pays and hands the girl a $5 tip. The drive-thru girl is pleased, smiles and thanks Leon instead of Larry. Leon smiles at her and waves. The drive-thru girl says "Wait!". The drive-thru window closes for a moment and re-opens. The drive-thru girl hands a bag to Larry to give Leon and says she 'put a little extra something in there' for him. Larry pulls away and into a parking spot to eat. Leon eats his burger (smacking his lips with each bite). Leon looks into other/extra bag and there are two desserts and the girl's phone number. Larry can't believe it/shakes his head. Larry pulls his lunch out of the bag and realizes his order is wrong. Larry is irritated and wants to go back to complain but looks at the drive-thru and there are a line of cars and refuses to walk inside to complain.

Leon (laughing at Larry): "You are one unlucky motherfucker!"

Larry looks at his sandwich...pauses, takes a bite and cringes. A large glob of mayonnaise falls out of Larry's sandwich and into Larry's crotch.

Leon: "One unlucky motherfucker."

Larry (looking in bag, yells): "No napkins!"

9. INT. LARRY DAVID'S OFFICE - DAY (FOUR)

Larry arrives at his office holding an armful of books and the box of chocolates. Larry puts the books on Antoinette's desk.

Larry (lacking enthusiasm): "Happy Admin Day!"

Larry hands **ANTOINETTE** the box of chocolates. Antoinette opens the box, notices the chocolates are half eaten and rips Larry. Larry apologizes, claims it must have been a 'manufacturing defect' and says he'll make it right. Antoinette looks at the pile of books and asks Larry, 'What are those for?'

Larry: "Never mind those...just something I picked up as a favor. Do something...anything you want with them!"

Antoinette tells Larry she wants to talk about getting a raise.

Larry: "Uh huh...I need you to do a couple quick things for me, first. Order Lou Ferrigno a new white shirt."

Antoinette: "Who?"

Larry: "Lou Ferrigno...you know...the Hulk!"

Antoinette: "Hulk Hogan?"

Larry: "No...THE Hulk!...the GREEN GUY!"

Antoinette: "Why would I do that?"

Larry: "It's a long story...I accidently spilled on him...never mind. Just order him a shirt...and you know that pedicure salon on Melrose...send the pedicurist 'Yashica' a box of chocolates and a Get Well card.

Antoinette: "Yah who?"

Larry (walking away): "Yashica. And why don't you order a box for yourself...Happy Admin Day. Do that for me then we can talk about your raise."

Antoinette: "Sure, Larry. Sure."

10. INT. LARRY'S HOME - DAY (FOUR)

Larry is wrapping up a phone call (unknown caller). The doorbell rings and Larry answers it. Richard Lewis is at the door holding papers. Richard says he just ran into Jeff and Jeff asked him to do him a favor and drop off some paperwork. Leon (in background) shouts to Larry that the horse race will be starting any minute. Larry invites Richard inside to watch. Richard and Larry sit on couch with Leon. All three are on the couch in front of the television. Richard Lewis sees the racing program and begins flipping through to get to the current race.

Richard: "You're betting these nags?"

Larry: I've got 'Bob's Weary' to win and Leon has 'Wet Claver'."

Richard looks at the racing program, studying the horses.

Richard: "Are you kidding me?...both look like plow horses. They probably stood in for Mr. ED or Budweiser Clydesdales...these nags would be lucky to finish one circle on the Merry-go-round at Griffith Park. Seriously, the only way these pre-dog-food mules could go a mile at the track is in the back of a pickup truck."

Larry and Leon banter with Richard about their horse picks. The race starts. Larry and Leon are both shouting at the television. Leon's horse wins. Larry's horse loses badly. Leon (jumping up and down/excited) shouts about all the money he just won. Larry can't believe his horse was dead last again and the tip he got from his 'insider' was bullshit.

Larry: "Fuck you, Bob's Weary!...you piece of donkey shit!"

Larry (upset), picks up phone and calls the 'insider' who gave him the tip.

(**Audio Dub**): "The number you have dialed has been disconnected and is no longer in service."

Larry complains about his long streak of bad luck. Richard Lewis laughing at Larry. Richard asks Larry if he recalls the under-cabinet CD players they both bought years ago. Larry remembers. Richard says he received a letter in the mail stating that tomorrow is the end of the seven-year extended warranty he purchased. Larry can't believe that it's been seven years and that his CD player has never worked properly and that he should have bought the extended warranty. Richard says his works perfectly. Larry recalls that they bought the under-the cabinet CD players the same day he helped Richard move into his new place. Richard reminds Larry how he broke the dresser mirror as he was carrying it up the stairs. Leon overhears this and tells Larry that explains his streak of bad luck.

Leon: "Seven years of bad luck every time your break a mirror, LD. SEVEN YEARS!"

Larry dismisses the claim but begins to think about it.

Larry: "If that's true, tomorrow, the bad luck curse ends and my luck will change!"

Leon: "Blah, blah, blah...let's get my money!"

Larry looks again at his losing ticket and tears it up.

11. INT. LARRY'S BEDROOM - DAY (FIVE)
Larry is in bed, waking up. The sun is shining brightly through the window. Birds are chirping. Larry stretches and says "Pretty...Pretty...Pretty Good!". Larry walks into the bathroom and looks at himself in the mirror and checks himself out up and down. Larry flexes his biceps (like the Hulk) then stands sideways to view his profile. While admiring his body in the mirror, the phone rings. Larry answers phone on nightstand. Cheryl calling to talk to

Larry. She asks Larry if they can 'get together'. Larry wants to know why. Cheryl is evasive. Larry agrees to meet. The call ends. Larry is smiling. Leon bursts in through the bedroom door and catches Larry by surprise. Larry tells Leon he should knock first.

Larry: "What if I was...you know!"

Leon: "Wackin' off?"

Larry: "No. I could be busy. Or Sleeping. Or undressed. Or..."

Leon: "Wackin' off."

Leon ask why Larry seems so 'happy'. Larry says he thinks Cheryl wants to get back together.

Leon: "That's one fine piece of ass!...You really fucked up by letting her go!"

Larry nods and says she just called him and thinks she has feelings for him again.

Leon: "I told you your luck would change!...I told you. Seven-year curse. Lifted!"

Leon says he (also) has news for Larry.

Leon: "LD, I decided to move out. Nuthin' personal, ya know, I jus' gotta have my own stabbin' cabin."

Larry: "A what?"

Leon: "You know, a pussy pad...and maybe even buy me a shaggin' wagon..."

Leon exits bedroom. Larry dances a jig.

12. INT. CHINESE RESTAURANT WITH JEFF - DAY (FIVE)

Larry and Jeff are finishing their (Chinese) meals. Larry tells Jeff that thinks Cheryl wants to get back with him and how his luck has completely changed after the seven-year-broken-mirror-bad-luck-curse lifted.

Larry: "I'm feeling lucky. For the first time in a long time, things are actually falling into place."

Jeff expresses doubt about the broken mirror curse but goes along with it. Jeff asks Larry if he's heard anything from the pedicure salon.

Larry: "No... but I asked Antoinette to send a box of chocolates to Yashica, the old Asian broad that I knocked out with my Bruce Lee kick."

Jeff (laughing): "Good idea with the chocolates."

Larry: "Let me ask you something...do Asians eat chocolate?...You never see an Asian eating chocolate...and you don't see too many fat Asians...Coincidence???"

Jeff (ponders): "You might be on to something...I can't recall ever seeing an Asian eating chocolate anything."

The server (Asian) approaches and places the check and two fortune cookies on the table. Larry asks the server if she eats chocolate. She struggles to pronounce it (saw krit?), shrugs and leaves. Jeff opens his fortune cookie and it reads it.

Jeff: "Look down at your toes...you should see all 10. What the hell kind of fortune is that?...Look at your toes?"

Larry (laughing): "Can you even see your toes?"

Larry opens his fortune cookie.

Larry: "Someone from your past will soon surprise you!"

Jeff and Larry (looking at each other, at the same time): "CHERYL."

13. EXT. LARRY, IN CAR, DRIVING - DAY (FIVE)

Larry is driving in his Prius. The phone rings. Caller ID indicates 'Cheryl'. Larry answers. Cheryl (audio dub) tells Larry she has something for him and wants to confirm their meeting. Larry starts guessing what the 'something' might be. Cheryl is vague and will not say what it is. Larry (excited) remarks about Cheryl being so persistent in meeting with him, confirms their meeting and ends the call. Larry stops at a Stop sign. A '**CUTE WOMAN**' crosses the street in front of Larry's car. Larry, with his hand out of the window waves, makes eye contact and smiles. The 'cute woman' approaches the driver's side window and asks Larry for directions. Larry helps her and she asks Larry if he would like to go out for a drink or coffee sometime. Larry agrees and she gives Larry her phone number on a small scrap of paper and says goodbye. Larry looks at the phone number and stuffs it in his pants pocket as he drives away.

Larry (looking at himself in the rearview mirror): "Pretty... Pretty...Pretty...LUCKY."

14. INT. LARRY's HOUSE - DAY (FIVE)
Ending, Part 1 – (Close-Up shot)
Answering machine at Larry's house is receiving a message from Leon: "LD...Ain't moving out!...pick up some food for dinner on your way home!"

<Fade Out> Pause <Fade In>

Ending, Part 2 (street scene)
CHERYL approaches **SUSIE** on a street in front of a store. They exchange greetings.

Susie: "I heard you spoke with Larry the other day ...about getting back together? What...are you fucked in the head?"

Cheryl: "WHAT are you talking about? I called him the other day because the IRS just finished my audit and now they are looking at Larry's last five returns...something about undeclared income---I just need to get legal document signed by him."

Susie smiles and nods.

<Fade Out> Pause <Fade In>

Ending, Part 3 (office scene)
Antoinette sitting at her desk opening her paycheck envelope. She examines the paystub and growls: "NO raise...Happy Admin's Day, my ass!...I'll fix him!"

<Fade Out> Pause <Fade In>

Ending, Part 4 (wide shot of nail salon interior)

An Asian girl hands pedicurist Yashica a card and box of chocolates. Yashica (wearing a head bandage) opens the card ---(on camera, the card is inscribed) 'Enjoy the chocolates...Larry David'. The salon workers gather around Yashica to look at the gift box. Yashica opens the chocolate box (the same box that was given to Antoinette) and picks up a half-eaten chocolate.

Yashica (visibly angry, in perfect English, subtitled in Mandarin): "Bald headed *ASSHOLE!*"

<Fade Out> Pause <Fade In>

Ending, Part 5 (interior shot, private home)

Lou Ferrigno at home, standing at a table, opening up a package. He removes an enclosed card and reads it out loud.

Lou: "Hulk...So sorry for bumping into you the other day. Hope you like your new shirt. Larry David."

Lou Ferrigno pulls back tissue wrapping and (with both hands) holds up a small t-shirt with the picture of the Hulk on it (facing the camera). He turns the shirt around and sees the Hulk picture printed on the front. Lou grunts, scowls, and rips the t-shirt down the middle.

<Fade Out> Pause <Fade In>

Ending, Part 6: EXT. PARKING LOT

Larry turns into a 'PAY-First' parking lot. The gate is already up and Larry enters without paying. A car in the first/closest spot is pulling out as Larry pulls up and Larry drives right in. Larry exits his car and announces: 'Yep, things are definitely looking up'. Larry closes his car door and is shown walking away in the reflection of the side-view mirror (camera close up on car door mirror). Larry reaches into his pocket and pulls out his cell phone. The slip of paper with the 'cute woman's' phone number (Scene 13) falls out of Larry's pants pocket (unnoticed) and onto the ground. The side-view mirror slowly falls forward and down/out of camera shot. Glass is heard breaking on the ground (Larry does not hear it).

FADE OUT/Cue Music.

(END)

Hearing Voices...

In the few weeks we spent pursuing a Hollywood/LA-based agent to represent us, we met a slew of people ranging from sleazebags to well-respected individuals. One agent was particularly memorable thanks to his unusual behavior.

A meeting with an agent named Keith began like every other meeting: simple basic questions. Eventually the questions became more in depth, requiring a degree of thought before answering...and that's where the interview went off the rails. Keith would ask a detailed question and before we (Ray or John) could answer, Keith would *answer* his own question...using a *different* voice.

We were startled. We looked at each other and around the room thinking a fourth person had entered. After a string of questions that Keith answered using the *different* voice, we excused ourselves to take a break and get some water. We were thinking HOLY water...for a possible *exorcism*.

It didn't take long for us to figure out that there was gold in the 'additional voice'/extra person concept. Scene 5 of the following episode brilliantly illustrated the gimmick. If you watch closely, you'll notice part of it found its way into Episode 10 (Season 9) of Curb Your Enthusiasm. (You'll also spot us (Ray and John) at the table behind Larry in the restaurant scene of that episode.)

Tying our extra voice ideas together required one more piece: We were sitting in one of those 60's-style throwback restaurants in Hollywood talking about the outline when John glanced up at the decorations and spotted an oversized life-like puppet. This was the vision that became...

Episode 3

"GUYS and DOLLS"

Synopsis: Duped into babysitting, Larry is playing *Mr. Mom* when he runs into a deranged ventriloquist whose dummy nearly drives Larry to puppet-cide. With Leon's unsolicited help, Larry quickly discovers who the real dummy is and the steep cost of parenting.

Scenes: 14

Cast: Larry, Jeff, Susie, Sammi, Marty Funkhouser, Leon, Misc. Restaurant Staff

Special Guest: Albert Brooks as the Golfer / Ventriloquist
(if you've never seen the Albert Brooks 'Deconstructing a dummy' bit from The Flip Wilson Show. (December 5, 1972), look it up. It's a life-changer.)

"GUYS and DOLLS"

1. INT. JEFF'S HOUSE – DAY (ONE)

LARRY, JEFF and SUSIE are sitting at the kitchen table chatting and drinking coffee. (Audio dub: baby crying). Larry asks about the crying baby noise and teases Susie of hiding her pregnancy. Susie says it's Sammi's baby and Larry quickly comments on 'babies having babies'. **SAMMI** enters the kitchen holding a loudly crying baby wrapped up in a blanket. Larry looks at Sammi, motions to hug her and congratulates her on being a new mother.

Jeff (looking at Susie): "There's only one *mutha* in this family!"

Sammi rolls her eyes/gives Larry an annoyed look and explains the baby is a doll for a parenting class she's taking.

(Shouting over the crying baby) Larry comments on how 'real' the baby looks and sounds. The baby is continuously crying (audio dub).

Larry (yelling): "Turn IT OFF, already."

Jeff: "There is NO off switch. You need to comfort the doll just like you would a real live baby."

Susie (shouting over the baby) explains that Sammi is taking a 'prospective parent' class now that she is in a committed relationship and has to take care of the baby for a few days. The baby has an electronic monitor recording its condition and Sammi will get a class grade based on how well her parenting skills were recorded. Sammi (frustrated) cannot get the baby to stop crying.

Sammi (forcing baby into Larry's arms): "See if you can make the baby stop crying."

Larry holds the baby improperly (banging the baby's head on the table/letting the head bob in every direction). Susie yells at Larry that Sammi will lose grade points if Larry doesn't support the head. Susie takes the baby from Larry's hands, comforts it, and the baby immediately stops crying. Jeff (motioning to Larry) says he can't take all the commotion. They need to leave immediately to make their tee-off time with Marty Funkhouser. Larry and Jeff leave.

2. EXT. GOLF COURSE WITH LARRY, JEFF, AND MARTY FUNKHOUSER- DAY (ONE)

Larry, Jeff and **FUNKHOUSER** are stuck in a fairway due to a slow foursome ahead. While standing there (frustrated), a ball screams past Larry almost hitting him. The **GOLFER (ALBERT BROOKS)** who drove the ball approaches. Larry criticizes the Golfer for not yelling 'Fore'! The Golfer insists he DID yell 'Fore'! Larry does not believe him and gives him the 'Lie-Eye-Stare'. Larry and the Golfer argue loudly. As the Golfer is arguing with Larry, the Golfer begins talking to himself/having a completely different conversation in the middle of the argument with Larry. Larry turns to look at Jeff and Marty and gestures towards the Golfer. They all are equally confused (shrugging). The Golfer is getting more and more animated in his conversation with himself. Larry breaks the tension by commenting on the Golfer's 'logo' on his golf shirt/sweater. The Golfer explains he's the owner of a high-tech manufacturing company that produces the latest golf clubs that will perfect anyone's swing, guaranteeing their scores will drop significantly. The Golfer tells them he travels all over the country in search of above average players looking to shave strokes off their score and that he is giving away free sets of golf clubs. Larry tells the Golfer that it's his lucky day (motioning towards Jeff and Funkhouser).

Larry: "We're all SUBSTANTIALLY above average players."

Funkhouser (quietly) tells Larry to apologize to the Golfer for the misunderstanding and offer to buy him dinner to secure the free golf clubs for all of them. Larry offers the Golfer dinner and the Golfer accepts. The Golfer hands Larry his business card and says he's free this evening and looking forward to Larry's call for dinner. (The Golfer drives away in his golf cart).

Jeff: "What a nut job! He needs a different hobby...like electro-shock therapy."

Funkhouser: "Who was he talking to during the argument? I thought I heard an extra voice in there."

Jeff: "He might be possessed?"

Larry: "Possessed? Repressed? Depressed? Repossessed? WHO CARES? We're getting new clubs!"

(Jeff raises his arm to give high-fives to Larry and Marty)

Larry (declines high-five): "Nah...I'm good."

3. INT. LARRY'S HOUSE – DAY (ONE)

Larry enters the kitchen and greets **LEON** (in the kitchen, frantically looking through the cabinets).

Leon: "How's the game?"

Larry: "What's going on here?...What are you looking for?"

Leon: "LD, this place is worse than prison...in prison they at least have food...all we have is...OATMEAL, FIGS, CHEESE THAT TURNED BLUE, STALE CRACKERS and SOFT CARROTS...this is bullshit, LD...from now on I'll be doing ALL the grocery shopping."

Larry laughs and mocks Leon about grocery shopping and agrees to let Leon handle it.

Leon: "So where are WE going for dinner?"

Larry (looking at his wristwatch) states he already has plans and needs to hurry to get ready. Leon (still looking in the cabinets for food) says he's going to the grocery store immediately and holds out his hand (for money). Larry reluctantly hands Leon some cash. Leon asks Larry for the telephone number to a limousine service so he can get a ride to and from the grocery store. Larry questions Leon's limo request and his champagne tastes.

Larry: "Uber it."

Leon: "Fuck that Uber shit Larry. I need to be seen in style!...Do you have any idea how many bitches are at the grocery store trying to get away from their punk-ass boyfriends and husbands just looking for a hook-up? I'm gonna find a sexy-ass bitch in aisle 12, buy a few porterhouse steaks, some good vino and bring her back to the crib for a little…you know…mmmphh (moving his hips forward and back)."

Larry laughs and mocks Leon's outlandish plan and demands the grocery money back. Leon refuses and wishes Larry a good night.

4. EXT. LARRY'S PRIUS – DAY (ONE)
Larry calls Funkhouser (using his cell phone in the car) and tells him he's on his way to meet the Golfer at the restaurant and soon they should have brand new clubs. Funkhouser tells Larry not to mess anything up and that he's counting on him. Larry reassures Funkhouser that he won't mess up and everything will be fine. Funkhouser continues rambling about Larry not messing up and reminds Larry of past screw-ups.

Larry: "ahhh…I'm going into a tunnel…you're breaking up."

(Larry presses the End button on the phone).

5. INT. RESTAURANT WITH LARRY AND GOLFER – DAY/NIGHT (ONE)
Larry, at the hostess desk, requests a table for two. The **HOSTESS** asks Larry if the other party has arrived. Larry looks around, does not see the Golfer and says "No". The hostess states she can't seat Larry at a table until the other party arrives. Larry argues/questions the restaurant seating rules but eventually gives in. Larry, waiting impatiently, watches other customers being seated. The

Golfer arrives holding an oversized suitcase-like box. Larry and the Golfer greet and Larry approaches the hostess and states his "other party member" has arrived and they can now be seated.

Hostess: "One moment while I check."

As Larry turns to say something to the Golfer, the hostess abruptly shouts: "David...party of two! Right this way." Walking to their table, the Golfer tells Larry he's asked a special guest to join them for dinner. Larry is confused and asks 'who' the special guest is? The Golfer says it's HIS 'guest'. Larry argues with the Golfer. Larry states that a guest can't invite a guest. The Golfer disagrees -- he is Larry's guest and the guest should be treated with respect and bringing another 'guest' is simply 'acceptable'. Larry is upset, but hears in his head (audio dub: voices of Jeff and Marty, "Don't screw this up. We're getting new golf clubs...") and gives in to the un-invited special guest. Larry asks the Golfer where the special guest is?

Golfer: "He'll be OUT shortly."

Larry notices the large suitcase-like box the Golfer brought. Larry asks if there are golf items in the box. The Golfer opens the box, pulls out a ventriloquist dummy and sets him on his lap.

Golfer: "Larry, I'd like you to meet my longtime best friend, business associate and special guest, **BUCKY FINKELSTEIN**!"

The Golfer makes Bucky Finkelstein 'talk' and introduce himself to Larry.

Larry: "You gotta be shitting me...THIS is your guest?"

Golfer: "We don't use language like that, do we Bucky?"

The Golfer looks at Bucky and Bucky looks at Larry (head turns and eyes blink). Larry (in disbelief) states aloud that he's having a conversation with a dummy! The Golfer tells Larry not to call him a dummy but to address him by his name...Bucky Finkelstein.

Larry: "Finkelstein? Bucky Finkelstein? The doll is a Jew?"

Bucky and the Golfer 'converse' with each other. Larry looks on (nodding/gesturing in disbelief). The Golfer reads the dinner menu to Bucky and they are discussing the night's dinner specials. The Golfer tells Larry that he's going to order the lobster tail and Bucky says he is going to have the Filet Mignon!

Larry (visibly irritated): "EXCUSE me?...Bucky is ordering a filet?...I don't think so! When I said I was buying you dinner, it was for YOU, not YOUS."

Bucky 'whispers' into the Golfer's ear. Larry is bewildered and irritated.

Golfer: "I'll tell you what Larry, I think we're going to say goodnight and leave, as you spoiled Bucky's appetite!"

Larry: "His appetite?...An appetite for what? Lemon Pledge? High-fiber saw dust? I'll let you in on a little secret...(Larry leans forward) Bucky doesn't *have* a stomach."

(Larry hears Funkhouser's voice his head again/audio dub: Funkhouser: "Don't mess it up Larry...I'm...WE are counting on you.")

Larry pauses for a second and apologizes to Bucky for the misunderstanding. Larry tells Bucky that his dinner selection is a fine one and if that's what he'd like to order, by all means order it. Bucky 'whispers' into the Golfer's ear and the Golfer tells Larry that Bucky accepts his apology and they will stay for dinner. The waitress arrives and takes the dinner order.

< SCENE TRANSITION – MIDDLE of DINNER **>**

The Golfer excuses himself from the table to go to the restroom as the filet mignon is served to the dummy. Larry (mockingly) asks Bucky if he can have a bite of his steak.

Larry: "Thank you, Bucko...that's VERY kind of you."

Larry cuts off half the filet and eats it. The Golfer returns. Bucky 'speaks' to the Golfer and 'says' Larry was eating his steak and was mocking him and his name. The Golfer is irate at Larry for taking food from Bucky and threatens to leave.

Larry: "He *SAID* I could have it."

Larry calms the situation.

< SCENE TRANSITION – END of DINNER **>**

The Golfer and Bucky thank Larry for dinner. (A 'Doggie

Bag' is in front of Bucky). Bucky 'tells' Larry that they will have to get together for dinner again real soon!

Larry: "Sure, Billy, Sure!"

Bucky (replies, in anger): "That's Bucky!...Not Billy!"

Larry asks the Golfer about the golf clubs that were promised for himself, Jeff and Funkhouser. The Golfer says he will be in touch with Larry within a day or two so they can arrange the pick-up of their new clubs. Larry (visibly excited) thanks the Golfer for the generous offer. The Golfer reminds Larry not to forget to thank Bucky as they are not only best friends but business partners as well.

Larry: "ahhh...thanks...*A Sheynem Dank**, Bucky Finkelstein!" [*-Subtitled- 'Yiddish: Thank you very much, Bucky Finkelstein.']

(Bucky looks/head turns and eyes blink repeatedly at Larry.)

6. EXT. LARRY'S PRIUS - DAY-NIGHT (ONE)
Larry calls Funkhouser from his car/cell phone and tells him about the bizarre dinner he had with the Golfer and his 'special guest'. Marty (audio dub) isn't interested in the dinner or the dinner guests and wants to know when he can pick up his new golf clubs. Larry tells Funkhouser that they should ALL have their new golf club sets in a day or so. Marty (audio dub) is amazed everything went so smoothly. He compliments Larry for 'keeping it all together' and continues rambling about Larry of past screw-ups.

Larry: "ahhh...I'm going into an elevator...you're breaking up."

(Larry presses the End button on the phone).

7. INT. LARRY'S HOUSE - DAY/LATE NIGHT (ONE)
Larry arrives home and walks into the kitchen. Larry opens several cabinets and finds them overflowing with junk food packages. Larry opens the refrigerator, sees all
junk food, and pulls out a few samples. 'Lunchables' are stacked from the front of the fridge to the back, String Cheese, Corn Dogs, Hotdogs, Jumbo Pickles, Whipped Cream, Jell-O, Popsicles, Summer Sausage, Ho-Ho's, chips, etc. fill all the remaining space.

Leon (enters): "Yo Larry...sup sup sup!"

Larry (looking at all the food): "What the hell is happening here?"

Leon: "I stocked up on lots of shit so we'll be GOOD for a couple months!"

Larry: "If we eat this shit, we'll be DEAD in a couple months!"

Leon (grabs a corn-dog, waves it at Larry): "Mmmm mmmm, love them corn dogs. Want one?"

Larry is disgusted by the corn dog and asks Leon about his shopping experience. Leon tells him he met two hot women...one in the fruit section and one by the frozen pizzas.

Leon: "I got both them bitches numbers!...I told you Larry!...this shopping stuff is like a daytime nightclub!...mmmm!"

Larry pauses, remarks about the grocery store being a 'daytime nightclub' and says it makes perfect sense and that HE will do the next grocery shopping trip.

Leon: "And go back to stale crackers and figs!...Fuck that shit. No Way!"

(Audio dub: a woman's voice is calling out Leon's name.)

Larry: "And, who's that?"

Leon: "Bitch in Aisle 12 – Frozen Pizza!"

Larry shakes his head in disbelief as Leon walks away with armful of junk food.

8. INT. JEFF'S HOUSE – DAY (TWO)

Larry is outside Jeff's front door and rings the doorbell. Jeff opens the door and greets Larry. Jeff hands Larry the golf club he left in Jeff's golf bag the previous day. (Audio dub: baby crying loudly in background.) Jeff steps outside closing the door partway to block the crying baby noise and asks Larry about the Golfer and the free sets of golf clubs.

Susie (in background): "Jeffrey?...who's at the door?"

Jeff: "It's Larry."

Larry (to Jeff): "What was that?"

Jeff: "What was what?"

Larry: "Your lack of enthusiasm...you said to Susie, 'It's Larry' in a shitty tone...you might have well said, 'It's some asshole'."

Jeff: "My TONE was Shitty?? What are you talking about?"

Susie appears at front door holding Sammi's baby over her shoulder (in a burping position).

Susie says hello and asks Larry for a favor. Susie wants Larry to watch Sammi's baby for the rest of the day. Larry immediately says NO/he's busy.

Susie (pushing the baby to Larry): "It's NOT like it's a REAL baby. JUST TAKE IT." (Susie gives Larry a barrage of verbal instructions).

At the end of Susie's instructions, she yanks the golf club away from Larry and hands him a diaper bag and baby carrier. Susie tells Jeff to get in the house and hurry up or they'll be late for the doctor. Jeff says goodbye to Larry who is standing with his arms full holding the baby and accessories and closes the door in his face.

9. INT. LARRY'S OFFICE – DAY (TWO)
Larry walks through the doors of his office (banging into walls/doors, etc. with the baby accessories) holding the baby in one arm (upside down). The baby blanket is dragging along the ground and the baby carrier is in his other hand. (Audio dub: baby crying loudly). Larry calls out to Antoinette but gets no answer. Larry sees a 'post-it' note for him on Antoinette's desk.

Larry (reading note aloud): "I've stepped away. Your production company visitors are in the meeting room waiting."

Larry: "CHRIST!"

Larry drops the baby carrier and walks into the meeting room carrying the loudly crying baby (audio dub). Larry wraps the blanket around the baby's head trying to mute the crying. Larry greets the **VISITORS**. They all look at Larry (horrified) as if he is suffocating/killing a real baby. Larry explains it not a real baby, and it's for a 'special project'. Larry convinces the attendees to start the meeting and ignore the crying baby. The meeting begins.
The crying baby gets louder (audio dub) and more distracting. An (overweight) exec/visitor motions to Larry to hand over the screaming baby. Larry slides the baby down the long conference table (like a beer glass on a bar) to the overweight exec (baby head bobbing up and down as it slides). Larry is discussing the baby with the overweight exec when he realizes everyone has stopped talking and is staring at him. Another exec/visitor announces: "Larry, this meeting is OVER. We'll call you to reschedule". The execs/visitors leave. The baby is on the conference room table crying loudly. Larry tries various ways to quiet the baby (baby talk, rocking the baby, burping the baby, reading to the baby, etc.) but has no success.

Larry's cell phone rings. Larry looks at the display: 'Unknown' caller. Larry answers. The caller announces himself (audio dub): "This is Bucky Finkelstein calling". (SPLIT SCREEN – Larry and Bucky). Larry asks Bucky whose phone he's calling from? Bucky tells Larry that he has his own cell phone. Larry tells Bucky that he can get brain cancer from cell phone use. There is a pause/silence on the phone. The Golfer's voice is heard (audio dub) asking Larry if he has plans for dinner this evening as Bucky and he would like to repay the gesture and take Larry out to dinner to talk business. Larry (visibly excited/swinging the phone like golf club) accepts the invitation. The Golfer is pleased by Larry's acceptance and states he'll make reservations for THREE at the same restaurant. The Golfer asks Larry about the crying baby he hears in the background. Larry says he's babysitting for a friend. (Call ends). Larry begins talking to the baby as if the baby is real. Larry realizes what he's doing and makes fun of himself for talking to a doll.

10. INT. LARRY'S HOME – DAY (TWO)

Larry (looking tired) walks in the front door holding the crying baby by one arm. Larry drops the baby next to the door followed by the diaper bag and accessories. The crying baby (audio dub) attracts Leon's attention. Leon (in a robe) asks Larry about the baby and the noise. Larry tells Leon he is babysitting for Susie's daughter Sammi. Leon tells Larry to shut the baby up because he has the 'Fresh Fruit' girl over from the grocery store and she just fell asleep.

Larry (looking at his watch): "She's sleeping this early?"

Leon: "Rocked that ass to sleep!" (Leon raises his arm to give Larry a high five.)

Larry (declines high-five): "Nah...I'm good."

Leon walks over, picks up the baby, says the diaper is LOADED, and asks Larry when he changed the baby last. Larry says he never realized the baby could crap and piss. Leon asks for the diapers. Larry doesn't know where they are. Leon spots the diaper bag on the floor and points to the bag motioning Larry to get a diaper.

Leon changes the diaper like an experienced mother while Larry makes fun of the baby's 'little Pee-Pee'. Before Leon closes the diaper, the baby gives a 'squirt' onto Larry's eye glasses (Larry jumps back, cursing; Leon laughs). Leon's grocery store date calls out (audio dub from upstairs) to Leon asking him about the crying baby. Leon yells back to her that he'll be right up. The **GROCERY STORE-FRESH FRUIT GIRL** comes downstairs and startles Larry and Leon. Larry and Leon try to hide the baby. Leon reveals the baby and the Fresh Fruit girl is irate (and says she hates kids). The Fresh Fruit girl storms out.

Leon (shouting after her): "It's not real!...It's a toy, baby...and you LIKE toys."

Leon (to Larry): "Never date a girl you meet in the fruit section of a grocery store."

Larry nods in agreement. Leon asks Larry what he's doing for dinner. Larry says he already has dinner plans--a business engagement. Leon tells Larry to bring him back a ribeye...medium rare, and a baked potato...(looks at dirty diaper), LOADED.

Larry (mocking): "Getting sick of those corn dogs?"

Larry asks Leon to watch the baby since he knows how to

keep the baby quiet. Leon refuses. He tells Larry he has another hot date scheduled for the evening.

Larry: "Another grocery store date?"

Leon: "Nope...Limo driver!"

11. EXT. LARRY IN PRIUS – DAY/NIGHT (TWO)

Larry is driving to the dinner-meeting with the Golfer. The camera pans across to the baby, sitting upside down in the front passenger's seat without a seatbelt. Larry abruptly brakes and the baby flies forward, banging/scuffing its forehead on the dash. The baby begins crying loudly (audio dub). Larry tries (unsuccessfully) to quiet the baby by talking 'baby talk' to it. Larry's cell phone rings. Larry looks at the display (Marty Funkhouser). Larry answers. Funkhouser (audio dub) asks Larry about the crying baby noise.

Larry: "I'm babysitting for Jeff's daughter Sammi —it's her baby."

Larry reaches across and turns the baby face-down in the passenger seat and pushes its head into the cushion to minimize the noise. Funkhouser asks (audio dub): "When did Sammi have a baby?" Larry explains it's a toy and that it's for a parenting class. Funkhouser asks Larry why he is driving around with Sammi's toy doll. Larry tells Funkhouser to forget the baby---he is on his way to dinner with the Golfer and expects to pick up their golf clubs. Funkhouser tells Larry they are all counting on him to get the new clubs to bring down their golf scores. Larry assures Funkhouser not to worry. Marty commends Larry for 'keeping it all together' and rambles on about Larry's past screw-ups.

Larry: "ahhh...I'm going into a men's room. You're breaking up." (Larry presses the End button on the phone).

12. INT. LARRY AT RESTAURANT/DINNER – DAY-NIGHT (TWO)

Larry arrives at the restaurant with the baby in the carrier (audio dub: baby whimpering; the baby's face is covered with the blanket). Larry greets the Golfer and Bucky. Larry tells the Golfer he brought a special guest and thanks them for inviting him and his special guest.

The Golfer (visibly irritated, repeats back to Larry): "YOU invited a special guest?"

The Golfer turns to the hostess and tells her he now needs a table for FOUR, NOT THREE. The hostess seats them at a table. Bucky, (appears curious/head turning/looking at the baby carrier), asks to peek into the baby carrier to see the baby. As Larry pulls back the blanket, Bucky leans in. (audio dub: baby cries). Larry places the baby in a baby hi-chair. The baby is wearing only a diaper (no pants or shirt). The baby's head is badly scuffed and appears dented. Larry 'whispers' into the baby's ear and the baby stops crying. Larry pretends he's having a (whispering) conversation with the baby. The Golfer tells Larry the baby is not 'real'. Larry glares at Golfer and then at Bucky and back at the Golfer. Larry continues to 'whisper' to the baby. The Golfer then 'whispers' into Bucky's ear. The waitress arrives. The Golfer asks Larry to order first but Larry refuses and insists the Golfer and Bucky place their orders.

The Golfer orders one meal for himself and nothing for Bucky. The Golfer asks Larry to order. Larry asks why Bucky is not eating? The Golfer (uncomfortable) says Bucky already ate. Larry tells the waitress to bring Bucky a Filet Mignon, medium rare, since he liked it last time, and wrap it to-go. The Golfer (uncomfortable) sits quietly. The waitress asks Larry for his order. Larry orders a king-size prime-rib and lobster tail. The waitress thanks them for their orders and begins to walk away. Larry stops the waitress and states he has one more order. Larry leans over to the baby as if the baby is whispering the order in Larry's ear.

Larry (caressing the baby's head): "Jesus would like the Ribeye, medium-rare and a loaded baked potato."

The Golfer is visibly angry and sweating from his forehead.

Bucky (turns to Larry): "You named your baby Jesus?"

Larry: "Yes...the King of the Jews! The King of Righteousness."

Golfer: "Where are Jesus' clothes?"

Larry leans over (as if the baby is whispering something in Larry's ear). Larry tells the Golfer that Jesus says he saw the Golfer's mouth move when Bucky was talking. The Golfer denies it. Larry announces he needs to wash his hands before dinner and excuses himself from the table.

< SCENE TRANSITION – Dinner is served/Larry returns to the table from the restroom **>**

Larry looks at the plate in front of the baby/Jesus (the ribeye steak is cut/missing half). Larry leans over to the baby as if the baby is whispering in Larry's ear. Larry tells the Golfer that Jesus told him 'you stole part of his meal'. Bucky 'whispers' into the Golfer's ear.

Golfer: "Tell Jesus THIS was his last supper."

The Golfer stands up (visibly angry) with Bucky on his arm. Bucky (turning his head to Larry): "You and your friends can forget about those clubs!"

Larry (holding baby/Jesus up, pointing to the Golfer): "Jesus said YOUR LIPS MOVED!"

The Golfer abruptly turns and walks away. Larry notices the Golfer did not take Bucky's to-go order (bag at table).

Larry (to the baby/Jesus): "Looks like Uncle Leon is having Filet Mignon tonight!"

13. EXT. LARRY IN PRIUS - DAY-NIGHT (TWO)
Larry driving (on his way home/after dinner). Larry's phone rings. Caller ID indicates Jeff Greene. Larry answers. Jeff asks about the baby and if Larry enjoyed babysitting.

Larry: "Piece of cake. The baby is sleeping like a log!"

Jeff is impressed and asks Larry when he last fed the baby.

Larry (repeats back to Jeff): "Fed the baby?"

Larry assures Jeff everything is fine. Larry tells Jeff he'll be over later with the baby after he drops off dinner for Leon. Jeff says it's 'getting late' but agrees. (Call ends.) Larry, talking to baby/Jesus, tells him what a good baby boy he is and how he is so quiet. Larry lightly pats the baby's head...then a little harder...then shakes the baby. The baby is not responding or crying.

Larry: "Long day...so much excitement...you must be tired. Uncle Larry understands."

14. EXT. GOLF COURSE WITH LARRY, JEFF, MARTY, THE GOLFER, AND SUSIE - DAY (THREE)

Larry, Jeff and Marty Funkhouser are on a golf course (on the green) preparing to putt. Jeff and Funkhouser are telling Larry how disappointed they are with him for blowing the golf club deal. Larry tries to explain by describing the dinner and the dummy named Bucky. Jeff and Funkhouser don't want to hear it and dismiss Larry's explanation as a lame defense of Larry's own screw-ups. Jeff turns to Larry and asks what happened to Sammi's baby and why he left the baby on their front door step last night.

Larry: "It was late and I didn't want to wake up Susie or Sammi, so I sent you a text message."

Jeff says he didn't see the text until 5am this morning, so the baby sat out all night.

Jeff: "When I went to bring the baby inside, one of its hands was missing and it looked like there were teeth marks in the baby's cheeks."

Larry says he doesn't know anything teeth marks or missing hands. Jeff said he put the baby inside before Susie woke up and hopefully she won't notice anything.

Standing on the putting green holding their putters, a ball screams past Larry, just missing his head. Larry looks all around to see who hit the ball without yelling 'Fore!'. Larry spots the Golfer approaching in a golf cart with Bucky Finkelstein sitting next to him dressed in matching (plaid) golf attire. Larry tells the Golfer he almost hit him and didn't yell 'Fore!'. Bucky 'asks' Larry if he liked *his* Filet from the other night. Larry turns to Jeff and Marty and gestures towards Bucky. Larry, the Golfer and Bucky argue back and forth over the bringing of guests to dinner. As the argument gets louder, Susie appears, aggressively walking towards them (appears angry/scowling, holding the baby by its single arm; Audio dub music track: 'For whom the bell tolls' by Gianni Ferrio). Jeff and Larry look at each other and simultaneously say: "Oh Shit".

Susie (in Larry's face): "WHAT the FUCK did you do to this baby?...Sammi not only got an 'F' for the class but we have to pay for this thing since you FUCKING KILLED it!" Susie throws the baby at Larry. The baby bounces off Larry and lands on the green.

Bucky (says to Larry): "You killed Jesus?!?"

Larry (to Bucky): "I didn't kill Jesus...He was sleeping!"

Susie (looks at Bucky, and then Larry and then back to Bucky): "WHO THE FUCK IS THIS?"

Bucky 'introduces' himself. Susie cuts him off and tells the Golfer to shut up. Bucky 'backtalks/trashtalks' Susie and mocks her while making fun of their inability to look after a doll. Larry and Jeff motion to the Golfer to STOP talking. The Golfer pays no attention to them and continues with Bucky's taunting of Susie. Susie gives a verbal lashing to the Golfer.

Susie (to Golfer): "Not *ANOTHER word* from you or the pile of lumber."

Bucky: "WORD."

Susie rips Bucky out of the Golfer's arms, tears off Bucky's head and throws the head at the Golfer. The head bounces off the Golfer and falls to the green. Jeff, Larry, Funkhouser and the Golfer briefly stand motionless/looking on/in shock, drop their putters and scatter/run in different directions.

Camera pans back to Susie ('huffing and puffing'), standing next to 'Bucky' (headless) and the amputee 'baby Jesus' doll lying on the ground. The camera pans and zooms in on Bucky's decapitated head leaning against the flag-pin over the 18th hole. Bucky's eyes blink once.

FADE OUT/Cue Music.

(END)

Pink Slip(pers)

In terms of inspiration for some of our writing, Art Pollacko (we call him *SMART* Pollacko) was a high point. And a low point. Art (SMART) was the perfect example of an innocent child trapped in a man's body. SMART was collateral damage from the crazed behavior of The World's WORST Boss (Volume 1).

When not tormenting us, the World's WORST Boss found time to push SMART/Art to the brink of a psychological breakdown. Neither Ray or John knew the extent of Art's condition until a tragic day in Los Angeles. John received a call from the World's WORST Boss asking that he meet Art in front of the office in LA. Art was a broken shell–living on the streets, broke, and confused. The World's WORST Boss, decided it was appropriate to send John to meet Art and take him to a medical facility rather than arrange for a trained crisis counselor. The situation unraveled to a far worse state during the next 24 hours, but ultimately, SMART/Art made it home and took steps to a full recovery. (And on a note of poetic irony (and karma), the World's WORST Boss, Art's primary tormenter, was given a 'pink slip'—not merely laid off, but outright fired).

During Arts steps to recovery, both Ray and John let Art stay at their houses while Art got his life in order. It was during those stays that they noticed two of Art's remaining and prized possessions: a set of Batman pajamas and a pair of pink bunny slippers. Letting a psychologically fragile person stay with each of us may not have been the SMART thing to do, but SMART's 'gift' to us was inspiration for...

Episode 4

"Fun_kHouse"

Synopsis: Larry finds himself forced into offering his guest room to Marty Funkhouser which lead to series of dark admissions *and* emissions.

Scenes: 17

Cast Larry, Jeff, Susie Leon, Marty Funkhouser, Antoinette, Sammi Greene, Wanda Sykes, un-named restaurant staff, un-named high school kids at sleepover (flashback).

Special Guests: Coffee Shop staff: Cuba Gooding, Jr; Betty White

"Fun_kHouse"

1. INT. LARRY'S HOUSE - DAY (ONE)

LARRY and **LEON** are sitting on the couch watching TV. (Doorbell rings). Larry and Leon look at each other. Larry gets up and answers the door. **MARTY FUNKHOUSER** is standing between 2 extra-large, overstuffed suitcases. Funkhouser greets Larry and enters the house dragging the bags through the doorway.

Funkhouser (smiling): "Thank you so much for letting me do this. You're a real friend, Larry."

Larry (confused): "What do you mean, thank you? Thank you for letting you do WHAT?"

Funkhouser's smile fades.

Funkhouser: "I'm thanking you for letting me stay at your house while my house is being fumigated."

Larry: "Stay here? I didn't know you were staying over. WHY didn't you call?"

Funkhouser: "I did call...your assistant told me she'd let you know."

Larry: "Yes, she said 'coming over'. She didn't say anything about STAYING over. Why did you call her and not me?"

Funkhouser: "I did call, but couldn't leave a message because your voicemail is full...you know, it's rude to have voicemail and just let the inbox get full and..."

Larry (interrupting): "How long are you staying?"

Funkhouser: "About 3...maybe 4 days."

Larry nods (reluctantly).

Funkhouser: "Maybe a week."

Larry sighs and is about to say something when interrupted by (off camera) laughter from Leon. Leon walks into scene with a drink in his hand.

Leon: "Wass goin' on, LD?"

Larry explains about Funkhouser and the fumigation.

Leon (nodding): "Foomy Gay...Fooomy-gation?" (walks away slurping his drink.)

Larry agrees to allow Funkhouser stay over. Marty's frown turns back into a smile.

Funkhouser: "See, that wasn't so hard, was it? Now give me a hand with my bags."

Larry walks limply toward Funkhouser's luggage.

2. INT. LARRY'S HOUSE - DAY (Two)

Larry walks into kitchen. Leon and Funkhouser are laughing (obnoxiously) while seated at the kitchen table. Leon and Funkhouser stop laughing and say 'good morning' to Larry.

Larry: "Yeah, yeah, yeah, good morning." (opens the refrigerator.)

Larry: "Where's my orange juice? I just bought a carton yesterday."

Larry searches refrigerator. In the background Leon can be seen raising the whole carton of orange juice up and drinking from it. Larry turns to see Leon taking a chugging gulp.

Leon (sets the carton down): "It was almost empty."

Larry tells Leon they need to set some rules. Larry tells Leon that he can't just take anything he wants, that he's a guest and if he plans on staying, he needs to ask before he takes something.

Leon: "Whatever, Larry."

Larry (to Funkhouser): "I need to go to my office this morning–I'll be right back–I'm just gonna pick up some scripts and the outline for a cooking show."

Funkhouser: "Can I come with?"

Larry: "Naaa, I'll only be...like twenty minutes, you don't need to go."

Funkhouser: "Why don't you want me to go, Larry?"

Larry: "It's not like I don't want you to go...it's just..."

Funkhouser (interrupting): "Just what? Look, if you don't want me to go, I won't go. I can stay here...away from everyone...all alone...by myself..."

Larry (sighs): "Alright...you can go."

Funkhouser (sarcastic/sing-song): "Thank you, Larry."

3. INT. LARRY'S CAR - DAY (ONE)

Larry is driving to his office with a depressed look on his face (camera only on Larry). Camera pans to Funkhouser smiling and looking happy, playing with the glovebox opener button and repeatedly lowering and raising the electric window. Funkhouser tries to engage Larry in a conversation, but Larry is unresponsive. Funkhouser continues trying to start a conversation. He asks Larry a series of childlike questions (favorite color, do you like Monopoly, don't you feel like playing stickball, do you want to play slugbug, etc.). Larry gets fed up after answering a few questions. Larry asks Funkhouser the same childlike questions.

Larry: "What's the most embarrassing thing that's ever happened to you as a kid?"

Funkhouser (starts to answer, but stops himself): "Back when I...never mind, next question."

Larry questions Funkhouser about what he was going to say. While talking, Larry is cut off by another car. Larry yells at the 'bad' driver and calls him a schmohawk. Shortly after the car incident, Larry arrives at his office. Larry parks, gets out of his car and tells Funkhouser he'll be right back. Funkhouser wants to know if Larry will leave the car keys. Larry declines and tells Funkhouser not to play with any of the controls in the car. Funkhouser tells Larry he will go inside with him.

4. INT. LARRY'S OFFICE - DAY (ONE)

Larry enters his office with Funkhouser. **ANTOINETTE** is ending a phone call. She hangs up and says "Hi" to Larry and asks Funkhouser how his house is with the infestation.

Funkhouser: "I don't know. I'm not supposed to go back there for a week or two."

Larry: "Did you say a week OR TWO???"

Antoinette (ignores Larry, smiles at Funkhouser): "Well, it's good you have Larry to stay with until you can go back there."

Larry (to Antoinette): "Yeah…. about that. Why didn't you call to let me know he was coming over to STAY?"

Antoinette says that she did call him, but his voicemail was full.

Funkhouser: "You see Larry, she DID call, but couldn't leave a message because your voicemail is full…you know, it's rude to have voicemail and just let the inbox get full and…"

Larry (interrupting, to Antoinette): "Why didn't you call my cell phone?"

Antoinette: "I knew you were busy with the whole cooking show thing, so I didn't want to distract you."

Larry: "Fine. Do you have those scripts I came to pick up?"

Antoinette says "yep" and hands him the scripts. Larry says "thank-you" and tells Funkhouser, "Let's go".

5. INT. COFFEE SHOP - DAY (TWO)
Larry and Funkhouser walk into a coffee shop.

Funkhouser (to Larry): "I need to take a Degner (pointing to the men's room). Order me a (complex/irrational coffee drink -- iced, non-fat soy decaf latte with cinnamon and no-sugar-added vanilla double-shot with room)."

Funkhouser walks away and Larry stands in line waiting to place his order. Larry steps up to the counter and orders. The **CASHIER** (**Cuba Gooding, Jr**) asks Larry if he'd like to contribute 50 cents for disadvantaged sub-Saharan African refugees.

Larry (pauses for a second and jokes with the cashier): "I'm not BUYING disadvantaged sub-Saharan African refugees, right???...OK."

Larry fishes 50 cents from his pocket and hands it to the cashier. Larry places his coffee orders and the cashier rings it up.

Cashier: "Your total is $6.50...*SHOW ME THE MONEY!*"

Larry (takes out his wallet and opens it): "Shit."

He looks at the cashier and smiles (embarrassed).

Larry: "I know this is gonna sound ridiculous but I'm...I...I need the 50 cents back---I only have $6 (showing his open wallet)."

Cashier (looks at Larry in disbelief): "Oh sir, I can't do that...I don't believe that's very holy...I mean...THOSE people need that money...and besides, I can lose my job."

Larry: "Come on (looking around) who's gonna know?"

Cashier (leans in close to Larry and whispers): "Jesus KNOWS."

Larry (laughing): "I don't think Jesus spends his time hanging around in coffee shops."

Cashier: "Oh sir, Jesus is everywhere."

Larry: "Everywhere? (looking around shop) Where? I don't see him? Is he here??"

A customer in the coffee shop with long dark, scraggly, hair and full beard-mustache turns in response to Larry's question.

Larry: "Is that him?"

Larry (to Customer): "Are YOU Jesus??"

The customer glares at Larry, turns and leaves shop.

Larry (to Cashier): "Not Him."

Cashier: "Sir...I'll give you the money back if you stop making our customers leave."

Larry smiles broadly. The cashier hands Larry the 50 cents. Larry gives the coins right back to cashier and walks away with the coffee (as Funkhouser is coming back from the men's room).

6. INT. LARRY'S HOUSE - DAY (TWO)
Larry and Funkhouser walk into Larry's house. Larry yells "Helloooo" to see if Leon's home.

Leon: "Wassup Larry...hey...Funker."

Funkhouser (corrects him): "It's FunkHOUSER."

Leon: "Funkhouser, Funky-monkey, Funky-brewster...it's all good."

Leon (to Larry): "Say Larry, do you have a spare DVD case anywhere?...'cuz I finished a movie and have nowhere else to put this shit (holding up the DVD)."

Larry says "no" and starts making his way to the kitchen. Larry puts his coffee down and notices that the phone is disconnected. Larry appears confused and calls for Leon again.

Leon: "Wassup, LD?"

Larry (holding up disconnected phone cord): "Wassup?? Did you do this?"

Leon: "Yeah, too many bitches were callin' and I couldn't take the phone ringing all fuckin' night, so I unplugged it."

Larry and Leon argue for a few seconds and the conversation trails off onto a different topic.

7. INT. LARRY'S BEDROOM - NIGHT (TWO)

Larry gets into bed and picks up a newspaper to read. The room is silent. Footsteps are heard (getting louder and louder). Funkhouser enters Larry's room. Funkhouser stops at the foot of Larry's bed with his hands behind his back wearing Batman 'onesie' pajamas.

Funkhouser: "I can't sleep."

Larry: "What do you want me to do about it?"

Funkhouser takes his hands out from behind his back holding up a book ("1004 amazing stories"). He holds the book out to Larry.

Larry (laughing): "Are you serious?"

Funkhouser: "I'm serious. It's not funny. Just read it, please."

Larry: "You're serious...seriously OUT of your mind. You expect me to read you a bedtime story? What are you, four years old?"

Funkhouser (in a serious tone): "It's not a bedtime story. My mother and then Nan would read me one story when I couldn't get to sleep."

Larry: "I'm not reading a story...you want a story? Here's a story...Once upon a time there was a little boy named Funkhouser who got thrown out in the street for not going to sleep. THE END."

Funkhouser: "Fine! Be that way. You're not a nice person, Larry."

Funkhouser walks out of Larry's room. As Funkhouser is leaving the room, Larry mocks him in a childish way.

8. INT. JEFF'S BUSINESS OFFICE - DAY (THREE)

Larry is sitting in Jeff's office talking to **JEFF**. Larry invites Jeff to go to dinner. Jeff says he can't go because he has to go see Sammi perform with a local theater group. Larry asks Jeff what play Sammi is doing and Jeff says it's West Side Story.

Larry: "No kidding. I just ordered a copy of that on DVD. I'll give it to you as soon as I finish watching it."

Jeff: "Great, she'll love to see it."

Larry tells Jeff about Funkhouser's fumigation/moving in/bedtime situation. Larry asks Jeff if he'd like to go get some coffee. Jeff declines. Larry gets up walks towards the door.

9. INT. COFFEE SHOP - DAY (THREE)

Larry walks into the coffee shop (same shop as Scene 5) and approaches the counter to order. (**CASHIER** is now **BETTY WHITE**). Larry smiles and greets her, 'Hello'.

Cashier (in an angry tone): "What do YOU want?"

Larry: "How about a 'good morning'?"

The cashier ignores Larry's comment.

Cashier: "Do you like sex and travel?"

Larry: "uhhhm...what??"

Cashier: "You want something OR NOT?"

Larry: "I'll have a medium decaf and (pointing)...one of those black and white cookies, please."

The cashier tells Larry the total due. Larry asks the cashier where the other cashier is?

Cashier: "I DON'T KNOW. He doesn't work here no more."

Larry: "Ohhhh?...I wonder if Jesus knows?"

Cashier: "Jesus?? WHAT THE FUCK?...It's $5.50. Show me the money or get lost."

Larry hands the cashier the money and leaves.

10. EXT. SIDEWALK - DAY (THREE)
Larry walks out of the coffee shop and down the street. **WANDA SYKES** approaches from the opposite direction. They meet and exchange greetings. Larry breaks the black and white cookie in half and offers the black half to Wanda.

Wanda (exploding): "Larry, why do you automatically offer me the black part? Is that some racist shit? The WHITE man can't eat the BLACK cookie? I suppose it's also not OK for the BLACK woman to have the WHITE cookie?"

Larry: "Uhhh...my coffee IS black."

Wanda: "Forget it Larry, Keep your DAMN cookie. And while you're at it why don't you go buy yourself some ENLIGHTENMENT and RACIAL sensitivity."

Wanda walks away. Leon comes out of a store in front of Larry and asks, "What happened?"

Larry (explains to Leon): "I just don't like the taste of the dark half...it's not racist."

Larry starts to give the black half of the cookie to Leon, then pulls it back and hands Leon the white half. The two walk away – Larry holding the black half of the cookie and staring at the white half in Leon's hand, Leon holding the white half and staring at the black half in Larry's hand.

11. INT. LARRY'S HOUSE - DAY (THREE)

Larry and Leon enter the house. Larry yells, "Funk?" but gets no response. Leon walks over to the couch and plops down. Larry is looking through his mail. Funkhouser walks through the door, announces: "I'm home", and starts walking up the stairs. Larry notices a book on the kitchen table and picks it up to examine it. He sees that it's Funkhouser's high school yearbook. He starts reading the comments inside the cover that were written to Funkhouser. Larry turns a couple pages and displays a perplexed/confused look on his face, looks upward /towards the stairs, and back at the yearbook.

12. INT. RESTAURANT - DAY (Four)

Larry and Funkhouser are sitting at the table finishing their meals. Larry tells Marty he saw Funkhouser's High School Yearbook, and couldn't help but notice the strange comments left by other students.

Funkhouser (looking embarrassed): "I don't know what you're talking about, Larry."

Larry: "It seems to me that there was a common thread going on with those comments...Pisspants?"

Funkhouser: "It's nothing. Drop it."

Larry: "Piss-Houser?"

Funkhouser: "It's just kids being cruel. DROP IT."

Larry: "Sheetsoaker?...what's that about?"

Funkhouser: "Fine, Larry! You have to dig up skeletons. I'll tell you this just so you'll stop bothering me, but you CAN NOT repeat this. (Larry agrees). When I was about 14...(*scene switches into flashback of a sleepover narrated by Funkhouser*), I was at a sleepover with a bunch of friends and everyone brought their own sleeping bag except for this one girl, Jenna Schmukler...we called her Slushmouth because...well, never mind, it's not important. I offered to let her sleep in my bag and she agreed. Everything was going great...until I...well, everyone was awakened by her screaming. She jumped out of my sleeping bag and someone switched on the lights. And there I was, in a sleeping bag soaked with piss. Of course, I ran away and went home, humiliated. And to this day, everyone I knew in seventh grade calls me those names." (*Flashback ends---scene switches back to Funkhouser and Larry at the table*).

Larry: "Wow! Does it still happen?"

Funkhouser: "No...It did happen once...a few weeks after Nan and I got divorced...maybe twice, so now if I'm worried about it, I'll wear an adult diaper to bed as a precaution. It's caused by stress, Larry, that's all. Just stress."

Larry: "And you didn't tell me this before I let you sleep on my guestroom bed?"

Funkhouser: "Of course I didn't tell you about it. It's not exactly the most inviting thing to say when I need to stay over at someone's house...and besides, I'm not under any stress, and it won't happen."

Larry: "Disgusting. The whole thing. No wonder you have a bug problem."

Funkhouser: "Larry...try and be a decent human being for Godsakes."

13. EXT. JEFF'S HOUSE - DAY (FOUR)
Larry is arriving at Jeff's house. He pulls into the driveway and walks to Jeff's door. He rings the doorbell and **SUSIE** answers.

Susie: "Hey Lar..."

Larry holds up a DVD (in plastic case).

Susie: "What's this?"

Larry: "It's the West Side Story DVD. I told Jeff I'd drop it off after I watched it. He said Sammi wanted to watch it."

Susie: "Ok, you wanna come in? I just made some blintzes."

Larry: "mmmm…Nah, I'm good."

Susie(pissed): "Is something WRONG with the way I make blintzes, Larry? Be cordial for once in your fucking life. Do you have any idea how difficult those are to make?"

Larry: "Not exactly, I just…."

Susie: "Fine, Larry. Act like an ass. I try and offer some hospitality and you throw it back in my face. You don't want my blintzes, then GET THE FUCK OUT."

Susie closes door in Larry's face. The door (re)opens, Susie snatches the DVD from Larry's hand and slams the door. Larry turns around and heads for his car.

14. INT. LARRY'S HOUSE - DAY (FOUR)
Larry walks into his house. Leon yells for Larry from upstairs: "LARR-AY. YO LARR-AY!". Larry heads upstairs.

< SCENE TRANSITION - *Leon's room* **>**

Larry: "What?"

Leon: "What-the-fuck, man. I put my titty flick in the DVD player and this singin'-in-the rain shit pops up…what-the-fucks-this?"

Larry (looks confused/perplexed): "AND ???"

Larry ejects the DVD, examines the disc, and realizes what happened (eyes widen).

Larry: "THE DVD!"

< SCENE TRANSITION - *Jeff's house* **>**

SAMMI is loading a DVD disc into the DVD player.

< SCENE TRANSITION - *Larry in his car, driving like a maniac, while holding his cell phone* **>**

Larry (into cell phone): "Come on, COME ON, answer, Jeff, come on, answer...ughh, voicemail. JEFF! Don't let Sammi watch the West Side Story DVD...it's a...it's a BAD disc. Don't let her watch it!"

Larry throws down phone, arrives in Jeff's driveway and runs from his car to Jeff's front door. Larry pounds on the door. Susie answers the door.

Susie: "You again. What now?"

Larry (looking past Susie): "uhhhmm, yeah...I need to get that DVD..."

Larry tries to get past Susie to go inside. Sammi is heard screaming from the TV room. Larry and Susie look at each other and run towards the screams.

< SCENE TRANSITION - *Sammi in the TV room* **>**

Larry and Susie arrive in the doorway of the TV room. Sammi's is backing away from the screen (*graphic porn onscreen*) with a shocked look on her face and pointing towards the screen.

Sammi (*pointing to screen*): "Mom...WHAT is that???"

Susie holds her in her arms to comfort her. Susie slowly looks at Larry (with outrage) and starts yelling/swearing at him.

Susie: "GET THE FUCK OUT of MY HOUSE and NEVER come back! AND TAKE THIS SICK SHIT WITH YOU, you sick bastard. WHAT the fuck is the matter with you? Giving this to an impressionable young woman? WHAT the fuck are you even doing with this?"

Larry: "It was a mistake—Leon switched the..."

Susie: Take it and GET THEN FUCK OUT (Susie throws the DVD at Larry)...you sick fuck."

15. INT. LARRY'S HOUSE – DAY (FOUR)
Larry approaches Leon's bedroom door and knocks. Leon answers/opens door.

Leon: "You got it?"

Larry: "Oh yeah...I GOT IT."

Larry hands Leon the West Side Story DVD case with the porn DVD inside. Leon takes out the disc.

Leon: "It's got a scratch on it, Larry."

Larry: "What do you want from me? You don't know what I went through to get this back."

Funkhouser (yelling from off camera): "Larry...I'm gonna need a change of sheets!"

Larry: "Jesus Christ. That's it. I'm throwing him out...right now."

Leon: "You get in that ass Larry!"

Larry walks to Funkhouser's room. Larry yells at Funkhouser for pissing the bed and is telling him to get out when he's interrupted by the phone ringing.

Larry (answering the phone): "Who?...Yes, he's here...Who is this? One second."

Larry (handing the phone to Funkhouser): "Make it QUICK. You have packing to get to..."

Funkhouser takes the phone and holds his finger up to tell Larry to wait a second.

Funkhouser (into phone): "Yes. When? Why didn't you call...I see. Thank you." (Ends call.)

Funkhouser: "Larry, that was the Exterminators. They said my house was ready two days ago, and called here to let me know, but couldn't leave a message because your voicemail is full...you know, it's rude to have voicemail and just let the inbox get full." (Larry scowls.)

16. INT. RESTERAUNT - DAY (FIVE)

Larry and Jeff are at a table, finishing their meals. Larry is telling Jeff he's glad the whole Funkhouser thing is over and he can relax now. The conversation is interrupted by Larry's cellphone ringing. Larry answers phone. Larry's expression conveys shock, irritation.

Larry: "Leon...Leon, slow down. When?...WHERE?...How many? Son of a...OK."

Larry ends the call.

Larry: "That was Leon calling to tell me we have bugs at the house."

Jeff: "Bugs? Like insects?"

Larry: "BUGS...BED BUGS!"

17. INT. MARTY FUNKHOUSER'S HOUSE - DAY (SIX)

(Camera angle pointing at the front door from inside the house.) The doorbell rings. Funkhouser (enters from off-camera) walks up to door and opens it. Larry and Leon are standing there, between 2 extra-large, overstuffed suitcases.

FADE OUT/Cue Music.

(END)

- 10 -

Pinocchio's Vagina

We (Ray and John) had encountered some memorable characters (liars) when we were still regular working stiffs. The World's WORST Boss-v1 (from Volume 1 of The LOST Episodes), as Ray put it, was 'a low branch on the evolution tree'. John was less forgiving: "He was a maniacal turd in a shirt and tie that should have been forced to leave the planet." It was after we left our previous jobs to become full-time writers that we began to realize how many liars, cheats, and pricks were around us—like zombies in a walking dead scene—co-workers, colleagues, and associates. This became useful to us when we accepted jobs in the TV and film industry. We were able to easily spot them and quickly avoid them. A bonus: the free 'material'/plot ideas they provided us.

An especially memorable example was this well-known TV Producer who was an abrasive, rude, offensive, twisted, compulsive liar, and generally, a worthless prick. But his true essence: Quid Pro QUO -- a reflection of his bizarre behavior. We casually watched as he awkwardly demanded sexual favors from young, talentless females as payoff in return for the (worthless) promise of a Hollywood opportunity. We were sure this prick was in line for a sexual harassment suit. At the very least, we were confident that the women he was lying to (and 'on') would figure it out and do something about it. WRONG on ALL counts. The prick repeated his offer to a handful of women over the course of the several weeks that we met with him. The women, it turns out, were trying to weasel their way into the business and willing to trade sex for an opportunity. Of course, he never delivered on his promises.

Ray nicknamed the prick Pinocchio. John reasoned that if the prick was Pinocchio, then the aspiring wannabe's were...Pinocchio's Vagina.

The more work we did in the TV and film industry, the more memorable characters (liars) we had to deal with. Some tried to do us harm (rip us off), while others simply told us lies. We weren't out to 'get even' with anyone. We were out to get ahead...without compromising or turning our backs to the truth.

To succeed we accepted the reality. There was truth and there was deception....and there was this immoral, backstabbing, conniving, snake. No doubt...

Episode 5

"What a PRICK"

Synopsis: Larry receives an anonymous office delivery that gets right to the 'point' and sends Larry on a mission to find the malicious sender. A thin-walled doctor's office visit stirs fear in Larry's diagnosis that causes him to live life to the fullest while exploring an alternate sexual 'lifestyle'.

Scenes: 13

Cast Larry, Jeff, Susie, Funkhouser, Leon, Larry's girlfriend Sasha, Wanda Sykes, Restaurant Staff; Doctor Morrison (Philip Baker Hall), Doctor's Staff.

Special Guest: Sasha Baron Cohen as 'The Rabbi'.

"What a PRICK"

1. OPENING SCENE – INT. LARRY'S BEDROOM – DAY (ONE)

LARRY is in bed reading a newspaper (ruffling/fussing with the paper in a noisy fashion). Larry's (Russian) girlfriend **SASHA** is in bed next to Larry, staring at the ceiling and gritting/clenching her teeth as Larry (loudly) fusses with the paper. Larry complains about the quality of current newspapers and how, 'after all these years you still get black ink all over your fingers when flipping through the pages'. Sasha interrupts.

Sasha: "Who reads newspapers? EVERYTHING is electronic these days...Larry, our sex life is getting boring."

Larry: "What?? I'm satisfied..."

Sasha asks Larry if he is 'OK' with adding 'toys' to their bedroom activities. Larry makes a few remarks about the types of toys ("radio controlled airplane" or an 'X-Box') and their function. Sasha tells Larry to spice things up or the only thing with an X (Ex) in it will be her. Sasha says she wants to hold a 'sex-toy party' at Larry's house and invite a few friends. She tells Larry's that if she sells enough products, she will get complimentary toys. Larry 'nods' but does not reply, looks at the clock, jumps out of bed and states he needs to go to the office. Larry gets dressed. Sasha repeats that she wants to stage a sex-toy party at the house as soon as possible. Larry (not paying attention) agrees and starts to leave. Sasha requests Larry give her a kiss goodbye. Larry mocks the 'goodbye kiss' rules. Larry holds Sasha's face in an 'exaggerated'/passionate way (with both hands) and kisses her goodbye. As he lets go of her face, there are two black marks on each of her cheeks from the newspaper ink on his fingers.

Larry (smirks): "Do you like football?"

Larry leaves.

2. INT. LARRY'S OFFICE – DAY (ONE)

Larry greets **ANTOINETTE** as he enters his office. Antoinette tells Larry that he received a special delivery and she put it on his desk. Larry proceeds to his office and sees a wrapped gift on his desk (it looks like flower basket). Larry searches for a card but can't find one. Larry tears open the wrapping paper and sees a large penis shaped cactus with long needles. Larry sees a card stuck through one of the long sharp needles. Larry scratches his hand as he tries to retrieve the card. Larry opens the small envelope and reveals the card.

Larry (reads aloud): "Larry, You are the biggest Prick I know!"

Antoinette walks in and sees the cactus and Larry holding the card. Antoinette asks who the cactus is from and for Larry to read the card.

Larry (reads aloud): "Larry, You are the biggest Prick I know!"

Larry tells Antoinette there is no name on the card and that he's shocked that someone would do something like this.

Antoinette: "Larry, sometimes you *can* be a prick!"

Larry, (ignoring Antoinette's comment) tells her that he's going to find out who sent him the cactus. Larry reaches to grab the cactus pot and accidentally brushes against the cactus with his arm and 'pricks' himself.

Larry (shouts): "Ahh...dammit, that hurts...and it's BLEEDING!"

3. INT. LUNCH AT RESTAURANT – DAY (ONE)

Larry and **FUNKHOUSER** greet and sit down. Larry is looking at the menu. Funkhouser notices Larry's arm is bleeding and asks about it. Larry tells Funkhouser the story of the cactus.

Funkhouser (laughing): "Larry, sometimes you *CAN* be a prick!"

Larry does not acknowledge Funkhouser's comment.

Larry: "It won't stop bleeding."

Larry says he's determined to find the person who sent him the cactus. Funkhouser, looks at the bleeding wound, says it looks inflamed and suggests Larry see a doctor as it may contain the flesh eating bacteria. Funkhouser explains the flesh eating bacteria and Larry appears visibly worried/anxious. Larry looks at his menu and can't decide what to order. Larry asks Funkhouser what 'looks' good.

Funkhouser: "Why don't you get the whole artichoke since it is filled with 'Pricks'!"

Larry is obsessed with his inflamed/bleeding wound and

says he's lost his appetite. Larry's phone rings. (Caller ID indicates it's Jeff.) Larry answers.

Larry (to Jeff): "You get the message I left?...Yeah, I got a little prick and it's bleeding all over the place!"

An elderly group of women turn to look at Larry and give him a look of disgust. Larry tells Jeff he's having lunch with Funkhouser and will call him later. (Larry ends the call.) Larry tells Funkhouser he doesn't want to talk about his arm anymore and asks Funkhouser a series of personal questions regarding his experience with sex toys in the bedroom when he was married to Nan. Funkhouser repeatedly denies knowledge or interest in the toys. Larry tells Funkhouser that perhaps that is why he and Nan got divorced. Funkhouser tells Larry he's lost HIS appetite.

4. INT. LARRY'S HOUSE – DAY (ONE)

Larry enters through the front door and greets **LEON**. Leon is wearing a white short-sleeve silk button down collared shirt. Leon appears 'excited' to see Larry and shakes his hand and pulls him in for a 'Handshake Hug' greeting. After the hug greeting, Larry looks at Leon's shirt and sees a blood stain. Leon looks down at his shirt and sees the blood stain.

Leon: "What the fuck LD...you just had your period/fucked up my new 'bitch magnet' shirt!"

Larry tells Leon about the cactus delivery and how he got pricked in the arm and that it won't stop bleeding!

Leon: "You should get that shit looked at Larry...all flared up and shit! Might be that flesh eating e-bowler or something."

(Doorbell rings.) Larry opens the door. (**WANDA SYKES** is standing at the door.) Wanda greets Larry then Leon. Wanda sees blood all over Leon's shirt.

Wanda: "What the fuck happened here?...Looks like a gunshot wound!"

Leon tells Wanda that Larry's 'prick' got blood all over his shirt.

Wanda stares ('wide-eyed') at Larry.

Wanda: "Why is yo' prick bleeding on Leon?...What the fuck's goin' on here?"

Larry tells Wanda the story as she pulls out a 'special' stain remover pen from her purse. Wanda rubs the stain-remover pen on Leon's shirt and the stain disappears. Larry is amazed that the pen made the blood completely disappear and suggests he use the pen on his wound to make it disappear. Wanda tells Larry he should take a bath in that stuff so HE disappears. Wanda hands Larry a black folder.

Wanda: "Here are your papers you left at my office the other day."

Larry tells Wanda that the black folder is not his --- his folder was a WHITE folder. Wanda accuses Larry of being a 'folder racist' and explains she gave the original white folder to her nephew who needed it for a school project. Larry comments the black folder shows dust and smudges and looks dirty and he prefers white folders for a 'cleaner' professional look. Wanda and Larry argue over 'black' being a 'dirty' color and 'white' being a clean color (similar to cars). Wanda tells Larry she's frustrated and offended by Larry's racist comments. Wanda tells Larry to go fuck himself and leaves.

Larry (to Leon): "Can you believe that woman?...a folder racist!"

Leon, (still) looking at his (stain-less) shirt in amazement, glances up at Larry.

Leon: "Keep your bloody PRICK away from me."

5. INT. LARRY AT DOCTOR'S OFFICE – DAY (TWO)
Larry is sitting in an examining room at a doctor's office when **DOCTOR MORRISON** knocks on the examining room door, opens it and enters. The doctor asks Larry if it's OK to come in.

Larry: "Come in?...you're already IN. Is that doctor etiquette? Why even 'knock' prior to entering? I'm the patient and I'm here to be 'SEEN' by the doctor. If the doctor just walks in the room without knocking everything would go much faster throughout the day and if you take each patient and count the number of 'knocks' and calculate the amount of time wasted, then your appointments would always be on schedule or ahead of schedule."

The doctor disagrees with Larry. The doctor explains that it is proper etiquette and polite. The doctor receives a text message on the cell phone he is holding (text message notification tone is heard) and 'reads' it. He types in a reply as he continues explaining proper office etiquette.

Larry (not listening to the Doctor): "I'm here to show you my bloody prick."

The doctor stops typing the text message and looks at Larry's crotch. Larry waves the bandaged arm at the doctor. The doctor nods, studies the arm/prick wound, and excuses himself from the examining room. Larry sits in the exam room staring at the closed door. The doctor can be faintly overheard talking outside the closed door. Larry approaches the door and puts his ear close to the door to listen and 'overhears' the doctor saying "Notify the family and let them know the prognosis doesn't look good...we will start treatment immediately but he will need surgery to prevent any further loss". The door opens abruptly hitting Larry in the head.

Larry (holding his head in 'pain'): "What happened to the etiquette knock?"

The doctor tells Larry he will prescribe an ointment for his 'prick' and Larry needs to schedule a follow-up before leaving to re-assess the wound. Larry questions the doctor regarding the conversation he overheard. The doctor insists Larry not worry and use the ointment to prevent an infection. Larry gives the 'Lie-Eye-Stare' to the doctor and says 'ok'. As the doctor is leaving the examining room (door open) he turns to Larry.

Doctor: "Larry, don't let a small prick ruin your day."

A nurse walking by the door turns her head to look and laughs.

6. EXT. LARRY (DRIVING) IN PRIUS – DAY (TWO)

Larry (putting his cell phone on hands-free/speaker) is talking to **JEFF** about his prick wound and how he overheard the doctor's prognosis through the doctor's office wall. Jeff 'accuses' Larry of eavesdropping on the doctor. Larry tells Jeff he overheard the doctor say his prick wound may be life threatening. Jeff suggests Larry start enjoying his life and do all the fun and wild things he's always wanted before it's TOO LATE (Jeff pauses) and asks Larry if he can have Larry's lucky putter after he's dead. Larry (annoyed expression) tells Jeff he wants to be buried with his clubs 'just in case' and he's already done all the fun and wild things...(Larry pauses) and begins telling Jeff about his girlfriend's sex-toy request and asks Jeff for his opinion. Jeff tells Larry that Susie likes toys and they take the pressure off of him to 'perform'.

Larry: "What do you mean, pressure?"

Jeff: "You know...it shifts the focus from me to the toy."

Larry: "So you let the toys do ALL the work?"

Jeff: "You, my friend, are a quick learner."

(Call waiting tone is heard from Larry's phone). Larry looks at the phone and 'sees' the caller-id indicates 'SASHA'. Larry ends the call with Jeff to answer Sasha's call (hands-free/speakerphone). Sasha (in an excited tone) tells Larry she picked up the toys for the sex-toy party and is hosting the party for her girlfriends tonight. Larry tells his Sasha that he's looking forward to seeing a bunch of women playing with sex toys. Sasha tells Larry both he and Leon are to stay out of the house while she hosts the sex-toy party. Larry (mockingly) protests but agrees.

Sasha: "Oh...I almost forgot to ask you, Larry...how's your prick?"

Larry (waiting at stop-light with window open): "My prick? It's STILL swollen and bleeding all over the place...and the doctor said it might be life threatening!"

An **ELDERLY WOMAN** in the car next to Larry (overhearing the conversation) turns and shouts (in disgust): "I hope your prick falls off...asshole!" and drives away.

7. INT. LARRY'S OFFICE – DAY (TWO)
Larry greets Antoinette. Antoinette asks Larry if he found out who sent him the cactus. Larry replies he still has no idea but sooner or later the guilty party will be found. Antoinette's phone rings and she answers. Antoinette tells Larry it's **SUSIE GREENE** calling for him.

Antoinette (covering the phone with her hand): "What did the doctor say about your bleeding prick?"

Larry ignores the question, walks into his office and picks up Susie's call.

Susie (to Larry): "Bleeding Prick, Lar?...You disgusting CREEP!"

Larry calms Susie down and explains the prick comment.
Larry asks Susie if she sent him the cactus.

Susie: "Why would I waste my time and energy sending you a cactus when I can easily call you a prick to your bald headed, four-eyed face?"

Larry tells Susie he will find the sender no matter how long it takes. Susie tells Larry the reason she called was to ask about his girlfriends 'toy' party tonight and how SHE ended up on the 'invite' list.

Susie: "Did my fat fuck husband put you up to this?"

Larry denies it. Larry asks Susie if she's going to the party. Larry makes a few blatant comments about 'sex toys' in the bedroom.

Susie: "It's none of your God-Damned business Larry! What the fuck gives you the right to ask those types of personal questions...You really are a PRICK Larry."

Susie hangs up on Larry (audible click). Larry stares at the phone receiver and then at the cactus.

8. INT. SYNAGOGUE OFFICE - DAY (TWO)
Larry is sitting with a **RABBI** discussing Larry's last visit to Synagogue. Larry tells the Rabbi his divorce and recent trips to New York caused him to miss 'a few' Friday night services. The Rabbi tells Larry that's no excuse. Larry convinces the Rabbi although he has not been at Synagogue, he has done plenty of 'mitzvah's'. The Rabbi

asks about these so-called 'good deeds' and Larry names a few bizarre examples. Larry sees a newspaper on the Rabbi's desk and attempts to change the subject by asking why the black ink they use to print papers always comes off on your fingers? The Rabbi gets back on topic with Larry and asks him to discuss the 'good deeds' he's done. Larry ignores the question and asks the Rabbi what his thoughts are on newspapers versus electronic media. Before the Rabbi can answer, Larry asks him what he thinks of 'sex toys' as part of a relationship. The Rabbi refuses to answer Larry.

Rabbi: "Larry, I reject the premise of your question."

Larry thanks the Rabbi for his time, stands up and extends his hand to the Rabbi for a handshake. The Rabbi shakes Larry's hand and sees Larry's blood-soaked bandage.

Rabbi: "Larry…What happened to your arm?"

Larry (opens the office door to leave): "It's nothing Rabbi…just a little prick."

The Rabbi's next appointment (a young **JEWISH BOY** wearing a yarmulke) is standing in the doorway.

Rabbi: "Very well. Take care of your little prick, Larry."

The Rabbi dispenses a spritz of hand sanitizer from a bottle and rubs his hands together. The Jewish boy does a 'double-take' at the Rabbi and Larry as Larry leaves the office. The Jewish boy stands 'frozen' in doorway with a wide-eyed expression.

Rabbi: "Come in...sit down. What should we talk about today?"

The Jewish boy turns and runs.

9. INT. LARRY'S HOUSE – MORNING - DAY (THREE)

Larry is getting ready to leave the house when Sasha shouts from upstairs asking a favor from Larry. She asks Larry if he can return the box of 'demo/sample toys' from last night's party to the address listed on top of the box. Larry hesitates to answer.

Sasha (shouting): "Please Larry? Those toys need to be back by 3pm or I'll be charged a late fee for them."

Larry opens the top of the box and carefully pulls out several bizarre toys that he can't figure out (holds them up/turns them around, etc.). Larry examines a red one closely. Sasha shouts: "Please Larry?". Larry (distracted) turns to look toward the stairs and places the red toy in his coat pocket. Larry reluctantly agrees to take the box. He (quickly) tosses the loose toys back in the box. An 'odd' squeak noise (audio dub) is heard from inside the box. Larry picks up the box and proceeds out the front door.

10. INT. RESTAURANT - DAY (THREE)

Larry, Leon, and Jeff enter a restaurant. Larry approaches the **HOSTESS** and tells her he has a reservation for 3 at 1 PM. The Hostess gives Larry a small red disk and tells him it will vibrate when his table is ready. Larry places the device in his coat pocket and turns to walk back to Jeff and Leon. Immediately, a buzzing is heard and Larry grabs his pocket.

Larry: "What was the point of the pager?"

Larry returns to the Hostess desk, (unintentionally) pulls the red sex toy from his pocket, places it (vibrating) on the counter and tells the hostess she 'buzzed' him. The Hostess (uncomfortable) stares at the vibrating sex toy.

Hostess: "Sir, THAT isn't ours."

Larry stares at it (vibrating) and shrugs.

Larry: "So...no table?"

Hostess: "I'll give you a table immediately if you will just PLEASE remove that...that THING from my counter."

Larry, Leon and Jeff are led to a table. A **BUS PERSON** is cleaning the table and wipes the chairs with a rag. The bus person wipes the table with the same rag. Larry asks the bus person why he would wipe the table with the ASS RAG? The bus person answers him in a foreign language. The three of them sit and Jeff notices a hand sanitizer dispenser placed with the condiments (ketchup, mustard, etc.). He takes a spritz. Leon nods in amusement. Larry looks at the sanitizer dispenser and tries to dispense some. The cap pops off the bottle and sanitizer sprays 'everywhere'.

< SCENE TRANSITION – food has been served **>**

Jeff is eating a shrimp and drops it from his fork onto the table surface. As he reaches for it, Larry cautions him not to pick it up.

Larry: "Do you know what's on that table surface? The busboy just wiped it with the ASS RAG….and you want to eat food that's been sitting on an ASS RAG wiped surface?" Jeff pulls his hand back. Leon nods in amusement and (quickly) grabs the piece of food off the table,

Leon: "TEN SECOND RULE."
(He eats it, making a 'mmmmm' sound while chewing.)

11. EXT. LARRY IN PRIUS – DAY (THREE)
Larry is driving and hears a car horn (behind him). Larry looks in his rearview mirror but only sees the top of the 'toy' box which blocks his view. Larry continues driving and sees the Rabbi (on side of road) waving at traffic for help. Larry pulls up to the Rabbi who is relieved to see Larry. The Rabbi explains he has a flat tire and needs a ride back to the Synagogue as he is late for an appointment. Larry explains he has to deliver a package for his girlfriend and won't be able to give the Rabbi a ride as he is already late but would be happy to call an UBER for the Rabbi. The Rabbi is very disappointed with Larry that he won't give him a ride and suggests Larry is not the good Jew Larry claimed to be the other day. Larry (looking at his watch) grudgingly agrees to give the Rabbi a ride but states they will need to hurry. Larry and the Rabbi are in the car discussing religion. Larry tells the Rabbi the good deeds he has done and how he is a decent person who helps everyone...when practical. Larry continues telling the Rabbi of his 'good and compassionate' nature.

Rabbi: "Larry, perhaps you could demonstrate some of that compassion---I need to find a place to stop...I have to take a Degner."

Larry turns his head and looks in 'surprise' at the Rabbi and asks if the Rabbi knows what a 'Degner' is?

Rabbi: "Everyone knows what a 'Degner' is...you know, a *CODE BROWN*!"

Larry says he doesn't have time to stop and locate a bathroom/that he is already late to drop off a package for his girlfriend, Sasha.

Rabbi: "Sasha? What an intriguing name."

Larry and the Rabbi argue about stopping as the Rabbi really needs to 'GO'. Larry refuses to stop and assures the Rabbi that 'he can HOLD it'.

Rabbi: "You know what, Larry?...You're the biggest prick I know!"

Larry (wide-eyed, looking at the Rabbi): "Ahhhhh-HAH! It was YOU that sent me the..."

Rabbi (interrupts Larry/shouts): "WATCH OUT, LARRY!" (pointing forward.)

Larry slams on the brakes to avoid hitting a car backing into the street. A loud screech is heard. Larry yells out the window.

Larry: "You fucking asshole!"

Larry turns to the Rabbi. The Rabbi is buried in sex-toys that flew out of the box during the abrupt stop. The Rabbi is holding a large mechanical dildo that has activated and is oscillating and making a squeaking noise. Onlookers approach the car, see Larry and the Rabbi (holding the moving dildo and covered in toys) and begin to take cell-phone pictures. An **OLDER WOMAN** approaches the passenger side of the car, reaches down to the street, brings up a toy (handing it through the open window) and speaks to the Rabbi:

Older Woman: "Here, Rabbi, you dropped your Strap-On."

12. EXT. STREET SCENE – AFTERNOON - DAY (THREE)

Larry is exiting an adult 'toy' store. Directly across the street, Larry spots a Butcher shop. Larry stares for a moment and then crosses street and enters the shop.

< SCENE TRANSITION – inside the butcher shop **>**

Larry points to large piece of meat in the display case (labeled "RUMP ROAST"--- the shape resembles two 'butt cheeks'), and speaks to the clerk.

Larry: "Yes, that one. And I want it shipped to this address with this note enclosed."

Larry hands the clerk a small piece of paper with the inscription: **'To the BIGGEST ASS I know'**. The clerk asks if Larry wants it delivered via 'express' or standard shipping and warns Larry that it may lose its freshness if sent by standard shipping.

Larry: "Send it the SLOW, CHEAP way."

13. EXT. LARRY'S HOUSE – MORNING - DAY (FOUR)

The morning sun is shining through the shades (birds heard chirping). Larry and Sasha are lying in bed. The camera closes in on Larry (reading the newspaper and looking at his fingers). The camera then pans to Sasha who is sound asleep (the top half of her face is obscured by a pillow) and smiling. Larry reaches under himself and finds a remote control (with a wire leading under the sheets). Larry presses a button. A low vibration/hum noise is heard, followed by a 'Tarzan'/jungle noise. Sasha moans in delight and turns over to face Larry. There are two black newspaper smudges on her face/under her eyes.

Larry (holding the 'toy' remote control): "Everything *IS* electronic these days…"

Camera pulls back/pans to Larry reading newspaper (lips moving with no sound). Larry smiles. Larry opens the paper/turns page. Camera closes in on the page of the newspaper facing the camera. An article headline is visible: **"Rump Roast Prank Poisons Local Resident"**

FADE OUT/Cue Music.

(END)

- 12 -

Whose FLEECE was White as Snow

We were in Los Angeles and Halloween was approaching. Ray wanted to take a woman he was dating to a costume shop to get her a sexy outfit. The costume shop clerk was on the phone when the three of us entered and we did a double-take at his conversation. The clerk, a 20-something clean cut white kid (who, it would turn out, lived in Beverly Hills) was talking pure gangsta'/hip-hop on the phone. When he hung up and asked if he could help us, his speech pattern switched to, as John put it, "whitebread, catholic school". Ray didn't hold back and to asked the clerk. "Hey, Eminem...WHY the voice?" The clerk never hesitated: "I adapt my approach to serve the customers. They could go to five different stores, but I *entice them* to come to this one". There *might* be an episode in this yet.

A sheep in its first year is called a lamb. Its meat is also called lamb. The meat of a juvenile sheep older than one year is hogget. The meat of an adult sheep is mutton.

We (John and Ray) were still in our first year of writing full time when a small writing job 'forced' us to work with a slightly more experienced writer---a hogget, as Ray would later point out. And we got fleeced.

The terms of the writing job we accepted required us to work with a large, overweight writer named Jen. Without outing her, Jen's last name sounded like 'Naverky'. We re-christened her, 'NO-Worky'. She had a nasty routine of asking us to review, critique, proof, edit, etc. her writing, though her real agenda was getting us to do the work she was assigned. We didn't catch on immediately, but soon enough figured out we were being hustled. The high (low) point of our adventure with this swindler turned out to be our last meeting with her.

We met Jen at a restaurant and after some awkward work-related discussion, Jen insisted on ordering appetizers. The appetizers (eggrolls) arrived as a serving of three. John passed the plate to Jen and she took two. Jen passed the plate to Ray and he looked at John. John looked back at Ray and said, "You take it!" Ray declined with, "No you take it!". Jen, being neither polite or slow said she would take the last one if we weren't going to eat it and without hesitating, speared it with her fork off the plate Ray was (still) holding. John mouthed to Ray: "Write it down!".

Eventually, we ordered the entrees. Jen ordered a side salad as her entrée because she 'wasn't hungry'...go figure. John ordered a full slab of ribs and Ray ordered a rack of lamb. When the entrees arrived, Jen commented on the presentation of both our entrees and asked if she could have a small taste. We moved our plates closer to her so she could cut off a sample. Faster than ninja bullet food processor, she lopped nearly half of John's slab of ribs and more than half of Ray's rack of lamb. We were dumbfounded. Jen proceeded to make the ribs and lamb disappear like a famine victim at an all-you-can-eat buffet. While we sampled the remains of our (now child-sized) entrees, Jen insisted she was skipping dessert as the salad had filled her up. A few moments later, Jen announced, 'excuse me for a moment' and stood up and walked away. Ladies room? Urgent phone call? Going outside to fart? No. Jen dined and dashed on us.

Especially in Hollywood, you can never be certain of who you are dealing with. It may take a few hard (or hungry) lessons to see through the con artists. While not a terribly expensive lesson, we had been taken by Jen. Her FLEECE may have been white as snow, but it also gave us...

Episode 6

"Larry had a *Little* Lamb"

Synopsis: Surprised by an unfit business associate, Larry learns the hard way that sharing is NOT caring. Things get out of hand when Larry has a run-in with a vocally 'gifted' individual.

Scenes: 13

Cast: Larry, Jeff, Susie, Leon, Bruce (the flamboyant cashier), sexy woman and friends, restaurant and coffee shop staff.

Special Guest: Roseanne Barr as Candace, the studio producer.

"Larry had a *Little* Lamb"

1. INT. COFFEE SHOP – DAY (ONE)

LARRY is standing in line to order a (specialty) coffee. Larry approaches the counter to place his order and is greeted by a flamboyant (gay) **CASHIER** (wearing a 'HI, my name is **BRUCE'** nametag).

Larry: "I'll take a cinnamon crapachino with…"

Larry pauses as he notices a promotion/specials board on the counter for a new coffee drink. Larry points to the board and asks about it.

Cashier (using an exaggerated 'lisp' speaking tone): "Oh, that's our new drink! We call it 'the swirly special'. It's absolutely fabulous. It's a latte with cinnamon, pumpkin spice, fudge, caramel, whipped cream and sprinkles!"

Larry: "Sprinkles??"

The cashier leans in closer to Larry and whispers (using an exaggerated lisp), "sprinkles". Larry orders the 'Swirly Special' drink. The cashier repeats the order to the barista using an exaggerated 'lisp' speaking tone. The cashier asks Larry for his name. Larry answers and pays. The cashier tells Larry (using an exaggerated lisp) 'Thank you, MISTER Larry! Please step to your left'. Larry moves to the pickup area. Names are called and (other) customers take their drinks. The barista picks up a drink cup, examines it, looks at Larry and back at the cup and says "Swirly Special for…YOU" and hands it to Larry. Larry takes his coffee to and sits down at a table. As Larry is looking at his coffee cup, he notices a cartoonish-caricature type drawing of his head (oversized bald head, glasses, frowning) with a 'stick' figure body on the side of his cup.

Larry glances at the cashier for several seconds, makes brief eye contact and immediately looks back at the cup. Larry looks (again) at the cashier. The cashier notices Larry looking at him and smiles. Larry looks away/back at the cup-drawing. Bruce (the cashier) announces to the barista that he's taking a 'break'. The cashier walks out from behind the counter and sits at the table next to Larry. Bruce starts to place a (cell) phone call and notices Larry looking at him. Bruce covers the mouthpiece of his phone and says to Larry (using an exaggerated 'lisp' speaking tone): "Sir, do YOU mind?".

Larry: "Let me ask you something...This drawing on my cup..."

Before Larry finishes his question, the cashier abruptly turns away from Larry and continues his call. Larry turns back to his coffee. Bruce continues his conversation on the phone (using exaggerated 'lisp' speaking tone).

Bruce/cashier: "Wait, WAIT. I have another call coming in. I have to take this. I'm putting you on HOLD."

Bruce answers the other call using a 'straight' (no lisp, lower pitch voice) and carries on a very business-like conversation. The call ends and Bruce resumes the original call (using the exaggerated 'lisp' speaking tone). The call ends.

Larry: "Let me ask you...I couldn't help but overhearing part of your last phone conversation...and I noticed your voice went from, you know...a 'gay' tone to a...some might say, 'straight' tone."

Bruce (in flamboyant lisp): "I have NO idea what you are talking about, sir. A gay tone? Just WHAT is a gay tone??"

Larry (using a lisp): "A tone...you know, 'fabulous'... 'sprinkles'...(returns to a non-lisped tone), you ARE gay, aren't you?"

Bruce: (without lisp): "I don't think it's any of your business!"

Larry: "See?! Right there! What was that? Where's 'The Voice'?"

Bruce: "The Voice?"

Larry demonstrates his point by mimicking a coffee order using an exaggerated 'lisp' speaking tone. The cashier denies using a different tone, says it is his 'natural voice' and accuses Larry of being a stereotyping bigot. Larry does the 'Lie-Eye-Stare' with the cashier. The cashier gets up from the table and announces (using a 'straight'/no lisp speaking tone): "My break is over. Thank you for spoiling it", and walks away.

2. INT. JEFF'S OFFICE – DAY (ONE)

Larry tells **JEFF** about his coffee shop experience and asks Jeff if he's ever wondered when and how 'The Voice' came about.

Jeff (using a lisp): "What? This whole thing? With the S's?"

Larry: "One day you discover you're gay and 'The Voice' is born?"

Jeff continues talking using 'The Voice' and carries a brief humorous conversation with Larry. Larry continues talking using an exaggerated lisp speaking tone. Jeff looks past Larry to see **SUSIE** standing in the doorway to Jeff's office listening to their conversation. Susie asks Jeff and Larry about the exaggerated tone of their conversation.

Susie: "This explains all those late nights...you and your lover, Larry!...Pathetic...both of you!"

Susie leaves the office. Jeff shouts using an exaggerated lisp speaking tone: "Bye Sweetie!" Jeff reminds Larry he has a dinner meeting tomorrow with Candace, the producer from the studio. Larry asks Jeff if he's met her before.

Jeff: "No. I did talk to her on the phone a couple of times. She has one of those deep, smoky, sexy voices."

Larry: "Like one of those late-night phone sex commercials?"

Larry begins imitating a 'phone sex operator' with a lisp. Larry wonders how attractive she is and asks Jeff if he should 'hit' on her if she is attractive.

Jeff: "If she's a not, you can always use 'The Voice'."

Larry finds the idea amusing and says he will try it.

3. INT. LARRY'S HOUSE – DAY (ONE)

Larry tells **LEON** about his dinner meeting the next evening and that he is meeting with a female studio executive. Leon encourages Larry to take her out for a
nightcap then make a move. Larry explains to Leon that she could be pretty, but he has his doubts since he has not met her before.

Larry: "Jeff said she has a sexy voice...but you know, the face NEVER matches the voice."

Leon tells Larry all big companies hire sexy women to attract business. He encourages Larry to dress a little less 'shitty' and introduce some color in his drab wardrobe. Leon convinces Larry to wear a bright colored shirt and tells Larry that 'pink' is in.

Larry: "Pink? I don't think so."

4. EXT. ENTRANCE OF RESTAURANT – NIGHT (TWO)

Larry (wearing a pink dress shirt) is walking towards the entrance of a restaurant and is trying to pass a large/overweight woman on the sidewalk who is swinging her arms wide as she walks. As Larry tries to pass, he is accidently 'punched' in his crotch by her wide-swinging arm. Larry hunches over from the pain and makes a rude comment about her waving her arms as if she were guiding in a jumbo jet for landing. The woman displays a shocked expression and yells at Larry for being careless and abruptly walks away.

5. INT. RESTAURANT - NIGHT (TWO)

Larry, enters the restaurant and approaches the hostess desk (limping/in pain) and tells the **HOSTESS** he has a reservation for a party of two. The hostess tells Larry the other party has already been seated. The hostess leads Larry towards a nearby table. Larry can see the studio producer he is meeting (**CANDACE**) is the woman that hit him in the crotch outside the restaurant.

Larry (mumbling to himself): "The voice NEVER matches the face..."

Larry is seated at the table with Candace. Larry greets her using 'The Voice'. The waiter approaches their table and compliments Larry on his pink shirt. Larry replies using a 'lisp'. Larry glances at a menu and orders a stuffed crown of lamb lollies. Candace frowns at Larry's choice and abruptly comments.

Candace: "I'm a VEGAN."

She orders a garden fresh vegetable platter.

< SCENE TRANSITION – dinner is served **>**

The dinner arrives and Candace stares at Larry's lamb dish. Candace comments on its amazing aroma and asks Larry if she can have a taste. Larry appears confused.

Larry: "Is the Lamb vegan?"

Larry hesitantly agrees to her request for a taste. Candace reaches over with her fork and spears half of the eight lamb ribs from the crown. Larry looks at his remaining (four) lamb ribs and asks Candace if he can try some of HER vegetables. Candace (immediately/forcefully) tells Larry 'NO' and states she doesn't share food with anyone.

Candace: "You never know where that mouth has been!"

Larry: "I may not know where it's been, but I do know where it's NOT going…"

< SCENE TRANSITION – dinner plates are cleared from the table **>**

The waiter returns and asks if they are having dessert. Larry immediately says NO. Candace orders the Bourbon-Bacon Cupcake 'to go'.

Candace: "It's not for me. It's for a friend."

The waiter turns to Larry.

Waiter: "Will that be TWO Bourbon-Bacon Cupcakes…to GO?"

Larry silently nods 'no' (in disbelief). The waiter leaves.

Candace excuses herself from the table and leaves. Larry's phone rings. Jeff is calling to ask how the meeting went and what does Candace look like.

Larry answers Jeff using the 'The Voice'.

Larry: "It's horrible. I'm completely out of place–she's certainly not my type."

The waiter approaches, places a paper bag on the table, looks at Larry, and says, 'CUPCAKE'. Larry hands him a credit card and the waiter leaves. Larry ends his call with Jeff.

A **SEXY WOMAN** sitting at a nearby table turns to Larry and compliments him on his 'hip' style pink shirt.

Sexy Woman: "I couldn't help but overhearing part of your phone conversation....and I noticed your tone of voice..."

The sexy woman tells Larry she loves his open 'L-G-B-T-Q' style and thought the waiter was rude with his 'CUPCAKE' remark. She and Larry chat briefly. Larry (using 'The Voice') tells her that was his good friend Jeff that called him. She tells Larry she is having a lingerie party with several of her friends and invites Larry and his 'special friend' Jeff, to attend since he obviously has great taste and her friends would appreciate a *modern* man's opinion of lingerie. Larry agrees. She hands Larry her phone number, smiles and turns back to her table.

Candace returns from the restroom (swinging arms wildly as she walks, forcing people in the restaurant to jump back/out of her way). As she seats herself, Larry immediately excuses himself to use the restroom.

< SCENE TRANSITION – Larry returns from restroom **>**

Larry returns to the table. As he sits down, he notices a small dab of frosting on the corner of Candace's mouth. Larry looks at the cupcake bag and back at Candace's mouth.

Larry (gesturing): "I think you have a little bit of VEGAN on the corner of your mouth."

Candace: "What? No, there's nothing there. (She wipes her mouth with a napkin). Nope. Nothing."

Larry: "You know what? I'm thinking I might want a cupcake 'To Go' for a friend of mine...let me see what it looks like?"

Larry reaches for the bag. Candace pulls it back. Larry and Candace briefly wrestle over the bag. The bag rips open and a single strawberry falls onto the table.

Larry: "Strawberry isn't VEGAN?"

Candace: "I've NEVER been so insulted in my life."

Candace stands and walks away (swinging arms wildly as she walks, forcing people in the restaurant to jump back/out of her way).

Larry (calls after her using 'The Voice'): "Oh, Candace, you forgot your strawberry..."

6. EXT. JEFF'S OFFICE – DAY (THREE)

Larry is telling Jeff about his business dinner with Candace. Larry tells Jeff she was rather large, not terribly attractive, hit him in his balls with her wide swinging arms and didn't apologize. Larry says he used 'The Voice' throughout dinner. Larry tells Jeff he was approached by a sexy woman who invited him and his 'special friend' to her lingerie party. Jeff (excited) asks Larry about the woman and sexy lingerie. Jeff asks Larry if he has knowledge of women's lingerie. Jeff insists he's an expert on women's lingerie. Larry says if Jeff will agree to act as his 'special friend', he can come to the party and look at scantily clad women. Larry suggests they dress flamboyantly. Jeff replies that may not be how the gay community dresses. Larry is not sure, but throws out a few ideas such as bright colors, plaid, shoes with no socks and ascots. Jeff laughs and says he'll have to go shopping and asks Larry if he can keep the clothing at his house---he doesn't want Susie to find it as she would kill him if she discovers he's come 'out of the closet'. Larry agrees and tells Jeff he will call him when he hears from the sexy woman. As Larry prepares to leave Jeff's office, Jeff and Larry tease each other talking with 'The Voice'.

7. EXT. LARRY'S PRIUS – DAY (THREE)

Larry is driving his car and receives a phone call. Larry answers the phone. It's the sexy woman from the restaurant calling to give him directions to her place where the party will take place. Larry quickly changes his tone to 'The Voice'. The sexy woman reminds Larry to bring his 'special friend'. She tells Larry her girlfriends are excited to meet them and help them choose sexy lingerie. Larry tells her that he's bringing his 'partner' Jeff and looks forward to it. (The call ends.)

8. INT. DINNER AT RESTAURANT – NIGHT (THREE)

Larry is having dinner with Jeff and Susie. Susie is standing at another table talking with some friends she knows. Larry and Jeff are quietly talking about the lingerie party (scheduled) the following night. Jeff tells Larry that Susie thinks they are going to a guy's-night poker game. Susie returns to the table and asks what they were just talking about. Jeff and Larry answer simultaneously: "Poker game". Larry asks Susie about the dark colors he wears and if she thinks bright colors are in. Jeff states he's thinking of getting some brighter, livelier shirts as well. Susie says both of them are starting to sound like a real 'couple'. Larry and Jeff use 'The Voice' to respond to Susie and the table of Susie's friends look over noticing 'The Voice' talk. Susie is embarrassed tells Jeff and Larry to stop it. One of the waitstaff is pushing a manual carpet vacuum around and under the table and chairs where they are sitting. The vacuum bumps into Larry's feet several times and the wait staff tells Larry to move his feet. Larry looks at Jeff and Susie but gets no response. Larry asks Jeff and Susie if they ever notice that restaurants vacuum when customers are seated rather than waiting till the restaurant closes.

9. INT. LARRY'S HOUSE – DAY (FOUR)

Larry and Jeff enter Larry's house holding shopping bags from their clothing excursion. Leon, holding and eating a chocolate covered banana, greets them and asks them what they have in the bags. Leon puts the banana deep into his mouth trying to scrape off the chocolate with his teeth as the banana slides out. Jeff and Larry stare silently at Leon. Leon comments on how good those bananas are and then asks Jeff and Larry to show him what they bought. They are embarrassed and refuse. Leon reaches into the Larry's shopping bag and pulls out a fancy bright colored pink shirt. Leon comments on how 'sexy' the shirt looks. Jeff and Larry look at each other and smile. Leon accidently gets a thumb-sized smudge of chocolate on the back side of Larry's new shirt. Larry is visibly upset and says it's too late to take the shirt to the cleaners and chocolate stains are difficult to remove. Jeff tells Larry the chocolate stain is low on the back of the shirt-tail and when he tucks it in, nobody will notice. Jeff says he needs to leave to take care of some things at the office and mentions he will meet Larry that evening at the 'Poker game!' and winks. Jeff tells Larry goodbye using 'The Voice' and exits.

10. EXT. DRIVEWAY OF HOUSE – NIGHT (FOUR)

Larry and Jeff pull into the sexy woman's driveway at the same time. Larry and Jeff exit their vehicles and admire each other's flamboyant attire. Larry has a bright pink shirt on and Jeff is wearing a bright yellow shirt. Both Jeff and Larry are wearing ascots. Both are wearing tight pants and Jeff's belly is stretching his tight shirt to the point of tearing. They approach the door and debate if they should be holding hands when the door opens or just act 'cool'. Jeff reaches to grasp Larry's hand and Larry pulls away. The door opens and Larry and Jeff are greeted by the sexy woman hosting the party. Larry grasps Jeff's hand and introduces Jeff (using 'the Voice') as his 'special friend'. Jeff and Larry enter the house.

11. INT. HOUSE/LINGERIE PARTY – NIGHT (FOUR)

Larry and Jeff are sitting on a couch (sitting straight and proper) when the sexy woman introduces her **Beautiful Girlfriends** to Larry and his special partner, Jeff. The girls are extremely sexy and Larry and Jeff are (visibly) excited to be there. The girls compliment Larry and Jeff on their bright outfits and ascots. Larry says they picked out each other's outfits. Jeff reaches for Larry's hand and thanks him for his ascot Larry picked for him. The girls announce they need help picking out outfits for their boyfriends to enjoy and tell Larry and Jeff to get ready for the lingerie show. The sexy woman tells Larry his pink handkerchief has fallen to the carpet. Larry bends over pick it up and the back of his shirt pulls up/out of his pants revealing the brown (chocolate) stain. One of the girls sees the brown stain and displays a horrified expression on her face. Jeff shrugs his arms and tells Larry he might want to tuck the back of his shirt in. Jeff and Larry watch all the girls parade around in skimpy, sexy outfits. Larry and Jeff have the women model the clothes in sexy poses, offering their 'expert' opinions. The sexy woman brings out a platter of appetizers.

Sexy Woman: "These are my legendary stuffed Greek lamb balls from my grandmother's secret recipe. Take two, they're small."

A platter of small lamb balls with toothpicks stuck in each ball, sitting on a bed of lettuce leaves is passed around. It's eventually handed to Jeff and he takes the remaining four (immediately eating two and holding the other two in his hand) and passes the empty platter to Larry. Jeff's cell phone rings. Jeff drops the used toothpicks on the platter and takes out his phone. It shows Susie's face on the caller-id. Jeff quickly excuses himself to take the call. Larry is staring at the empty platter and lifts a lettuce leaf in search for a lamb ball.

< SCENE TRANSITION – Jeff is in a dimly lit bedroom, answering his phone **>**

Jeff, in the back bedroom is quietly 'sweet talking' Susie. Susie (not heard) asks Jeff when he will be home and Jeff in a low tone of voice tells her he won't be late. One of the girls is in the adjacent bathroom changing into another lingerie outfit and overhears Jeff's phone conversation. She accuses him of cheating on Larry, becomes irate and leaves the bedroom.

< **SCENE TRANSITION** – Living-room with Larry and Lingerie Girls >

The girl (from the back bedroom-bathroom) enters the living room where the others are and tells them Larry's partner Jeff is CHEATING! She tells everyone she just caught Jeff talking to another lover on the phone. Jeff returns to the living room and the women begin telling Jeff off and suggest to Larry that he dump him. Larry acts out a breakup scene, dumps Jeff and demands he leave immediately. Jeff (confused) agrees to leave. Larry, acting visibly upset and attempting to cry is comforted by the beautiful women. The women assure Larry not to worry as they can help him to find love again. Larry tries to say he doesn't need 'love' but the girls (dressed in their skimpy lingerie) are insistent and give Larry a group hug.

12. INT. JEFF'S OFFICE – DAY (FIVE)
Larry is talking to Jeff about their 'breakup'. Jeff tells Larry during the night of the lingerie show, he was talking to Susie in the back bedroom and didn't notice there was another girl in the room. Jeff thinks she must have thought he was talking to another man. Larry tells Jeff the girls were hugging him all night to comfort him and all was going great until they promised to help him find a new partner. Jeff asks Larry how he's going to handle that. Larry admits that he doesn't have a plan.

Jeff (using 'The Voice'): "Your ass is grass mister!"

Larry's cell phone rings and Larry answers. It's the sexy woman calling to check on Larry. Larry forgets to use 'The Voice' but quickly adjusts. She tells Larry she has a nice surprise for him and wants to meet at the coffee shop on 8th Street to reveal the surprise. Larry tells her he knows the place well and can be their shortly.

13. INT. COFFEE SHOP – DAY (FOUR)

Larry, enters the coffee shop (same shop as/from scene 1) and sees the sexy woman sitting at a table with her coffee. Larry greets the sexy woman. She gives Larry a long exaggerated hug, consoling him about his recent breakup. Larry acts broken-up from the loss and enjoys the attention from the sexy woman. She asks Larry if he's ready for his big surprise. Larry (enthusiastically) agrees. She asks Larry to stand up, cover his eyes and not to peek. Larry stands patiently covering his eyes with his hand. The sexy woman tells Larry to hold out his other hand and wait for a moment. The sexy woman puts the hand of an unseen individual into Larry's hand and tells them both they can now open their eyes. Larry is holding hands with and looking directly into the eyes of the flamboyant cashier (from scene 1).

Sexy woman: "Larry, I'd like you to meet my brother, Bruce..."

Cue Music.

[Camera closes in on coffee shop promotion/specials board on the counter (visible behind Bruce). The board is illustrated with a cartoonish-caricature type drawing.]

APERTURE FADE OUT.

(END)

14

Daylight at the End of the Rectum

Have you ever noticed when you go to the doctor, they're always trying to stick things up your ass? Fingers, instruments, cameras, drugs (the legal/prescription type, that is), it's always something. Then, there was this dentist...let's not go into that one. Still, Ray and John were keeping up-to-date health-wise. With squeaky clean colons and teeth as white as albino iguanas, things were looking up.

We were being solicited for input on TV projects by anybody and everybody. Naturally, they all thought the material they had was THE GREATEST. The GREATEST! What isn't the GREATEST these days? We're constantly urged to try 'the world's finest salad bar', or 'the world's best steak knives', and even 'the worlds' greatest toilet paper'. ENOUGH!

While some of the material we saw may have had potential, we used most of what we received to level out wobbly table legs at outdoor cafes in Manhattan Beach. We were getting piles of material in the mail as well...made for excellent liners in the dog cage. Over and over, people would claim to have The GREATEST idea/concept/treatment and wanted our help to 'fill in some gaps'. Gaps? Holes so big that
NASA could send a deep space probe into it and it wouldn't come back for a century.

Regardless, it was promising. We were getting writing offers which encouraged us. Those small 'encouragements' were eclipsed by getting THE CALL. An executive producer for Curb Your Enthusiasm had read our material and called, wanting to talk with us. The vagueness of the emails, voicemails and phone conversations were unsettling. The producer wouldn't tell us specifically what the discussion was going to be about. For all we knew, we were being asked to fly to Los Angeles so that we could be handed a cease and desist order. It turned out for the best. They were interested in our material and wanted to know if we would be interested in meeting the rest of the Curb Your Enthusiasm production company.

We endured a lot. Was it possible that we would go from working for the WORLD'S WORST Boss to writing standup and books to working on one of the world's GREATEST comedy series? This may be our big break --- the light at the end of the tunnel. But we will NEVER forget the evil behavior that inspired us...

15

Episode 7

"World's Greatest Asshole"

Synopsis: A visit to the dentist's office goes downhill as Larry's mouth gets him into trouble. Larry tries his hand in interracial flirting and has an unexpected run in with one of the world's greatest Olympians.

Scenes: 22

Cast: Larry, Jeff, Susie, Leon, Sammi, Ted, Mary, Disabled man, Disabled man's caretaker, Attractive black woman, Man in pickup truck.

Special Guests: Caitlyn Jenner; Dustin Hoffman as the Dentist.

"World's Greatest Asshole"

1. INT. DENTIST'S OFFICE – SITTING IN EXAMINATION CHAIR – DAY (ONE)

LARRY is sitting in the dentist's chair looking at and playing with the dentist's tools. The **DENTIST** walks in and greets Larry. He asks Larry if he's been playing with his tools. Larry denies it. The dentist briefly gives Larry the 'Lie-Eye-Stare'. As they converse, the dentist begins his work. While Larry is getting his teeth cleaned, the dentist asks him questions. Larry is unable to give a clear response because his mouth is open and being worked on. Larry mockingly responds in a series of grunts, and enthused gibberish, while moving his hands in fake excitement. Larry is finally able to close his mouth and talk as the dentist is switching tools, "You know, it's a little hard to talk while your hands are in my mouth." The dentist jokingly says he's "been doing this for so long, you begin to understand the gibberish." They both laugh and the dentist proceeds with the cleaning.

2. INT. DENTIST'S OFFICE – SITTING IN EXAMINATION CHAIR – LATER DAY (ONE)

The doctor has finished cleaning Larry's teeth and has left the room. Larry begins to look around the room and observes a coffee mug that says, "WORLD'S GREATEST DOCTOR!" He scoffs and shakes his head. The dentist comes back to the room and says, "Well, everything looks good Mr. David! Clean as a whistle. You..." Larry interrupts the dentist by pointing to the mug.

Larry: "WORLD'S GREATEST DOCTOR?"

Dentist: "Oh, isn't that cute? My daughter got it for me."

Larry asks about the title on the mug, "Doctor"? The dentist responds, "Yep", and points to his degree on the wall.

Larry (laughing): "You brush people's teeth and that makes you a doctor? By that logic, I'm also a doctor, right?"

Dentist (sternly): "I AM a licensed PHYSICIAN!"

Larry (corrects him) "DENTIST."

Dentist (visibly annoyed): "We're going need to do some X-rays and you'll be on your way, Mr. David."

The dentist leaves the room.

Larry (mocking): "OK DOCTOR. WHATEVER YOU SAY DOCTOR. OH EXCUSE ME NURSE, CAN YOU HAND ME MY TOOTHBRUSH? SURE THING, DOCTOR!"

The dentist comes back in with a small lead vest and puts it around Larry's neck. Larry looks down and sees that the vest only goes down to just below his belly button.

Larry questions the length of the vest.

Larry: "IS IT SAFE? Shouldn't we be using the ADULT size vest, DOCTOR?"

Dentist (dismissively): "Yes, it's safe. It's very safe, It's so safe you wouldn't believe it."

Larry tries to pull the vest down over his genitals. The

dentist moves the X-Ray machine up to Larry's face and pulls the vest up. Before Larry can pull the vest down over his waist, the dentist pushes Larry back in the chair and says, "Sit still, let's take a look at those molars." Larry looks up into the camera with a worried look on his face (audio dub: rapid click of the X-ray machine).

(Cue Intro Music)

3. INT. JEFF'S HOUSE – SITTING AT TABLE – DAY (ONE)

Larry is telling **JEFF** about his dentist office experience and the X-ray vest.

Jeff (laughing at Larry): "It's not exactly like you're in the prime of your life, what are you worried about? You had like 4 sperm before, now you have 3, what's the big deal?"

Larry (defensive): "Hey, it was a strong 4, now I'm down to the *lone ranger*."

Jeff: "It's not like you're going to have kids...and, you've got your sponsored kid, David David...but that's different."

They both laugh. Jeff reminds Larry that Susie's birthday party is in a couple of days. Larry asks what he should get her and Jeff 'jokingly' says, "A muzzle." Larry and Jeff agree to go out for lunch and leave.

4. INT. RESTAURANT – WAITING FOR TABLE – DAY (ONE)

Larry and Jeff are standing in the waiting area of a restaurant. Larry notices an **ATTRACTIVE BLACK**

WOMAN standing alone. Larry nudges Jeff and nods his head toward her.

Jeff: "You like her? Go talk to her."

Larry says he can't because his 'moves' won't work on her. Jeff questions Larry. Larry tells Jeff his 'moves' are designed for middle-aged Caucasian women. Jeff laughs and tells Larry to try something new and Larry agrees. He walks over to her and strikes up a conversation. She politely engages in small talk with Larry but appears uninterested. Larry excuses himself and walks back to Jeff shrugging his shoulders. Larry says, "You see?". The hostess takes Jeff and Larry to their table.

5. INT. RESTAURANT – SITTING AT TABLE – DAY (ONE)

Shortly after they sit down, a **DISABLED MAN** in a motorized chair rolls past their table. After he passes their table, he stops, puts his chair in reverse and backs up. He stops next to Larry. Larry notices the man has a small piece of paper sticking out of his pocket. The disabled man politely asks Larry to take his (disabled man's) phone out of his pocket, as he is unable to do it himself because of his disability. Larry agrees ("Okay"), reaches into the disabled man's shirt pocket, and pulls out a phone. He asks Larry if he could take the piece of paper out from his pocket and call the phone number written on it. Larry dials the number and the disabled man asks Larry to hold the phone up to his ear. Larry holds the phone up to the disabled man's ear as he makes the call. The disabled man's phone conversation starts out normal but rapidly changes as he starts yelling and cursing at the person that was called. Larry looks over at Jeff and they both shrug. The phone conversation ends with the disabled man shouting "FUCK YOU!". He turns to Larry and tells him to "angrily hang up the phone." He calms down (immediately) and apologizes to Larry about the nature of his phone call. He explains that his ex-wife is a "bitch" and makes a series of vulgar comments about her. With each comment, he appears to get more angry.

Disabled man (to Larry): "You know what? I want you to text her right now!"

Larry: "What? You want me to do what?"

Disabled man: "Text her, yeah, tell her she's a..." (shouts a list of obscenities).

Larry is seen texting them out. As Larry types the last obscenity, the **DISABLED MAN'S CARETAKER** walks up and asks, "What's going on here?" and looks at Larry holding the man's phone.

Larry: "Who are you?"

Caretaker: "I'm his caretaker!"

He grabs the phone from Larry's hand and starts to read (out loud) the texts that Larry sent. The caretaker yells at Larry for texting the disabled man's ex-wife. (Larry is unable to get a word in to explain.) The caretaker tells Larry he should be ashamed of himself and leaves with the disabled man. Jeff and Larry both look at each other in shock and confusion. They quietly discuss the situation. A

WAITER appears and greets them. The waiter politely asks if they'd like to hear the specials. Larry (abruptly) says, "No thanks, we're good." The waiter proceeds to list off the specials, "Well, we have herb encrusted salmon with a Russian..." Larry raises his hands at the waiter. The waiter stops reciting the specials and asks Larry, "Is there a problem?"

Larry: "As a matter of fact, there *is* a problem. I told you I don't want to hear the specials, and you proceeded to list them out. Did I..."

Waiter (interrupting): "It's our policy, I have to describe the specials to the customers as a..."

Larry (interrupting) "Then why ask? Why go through the trouble of asking me if you have to read them out anyway? Your logic doesn't make sense."

The argument ends with both agreeing in makes 'no sense'. Jeff orders a chef salad. Larry (mumbles to himself): "Salmon...salmon...Rushdie." Larry orders the herb encrusted salmon that the waiter listed as the daily 'special'.

6. INT. LARRY'S OFFICE – SITTING AT DESK – DAY (ONE)
Larry is on the phone, arranging lunch plans with Ted and Mary. They both agree on where they are having lunch "tomorrow" and end the conversation. Larry briefly plays with a Rubik's cube on his desk and leaves his office (heading for the bathroom).

7. INT. LARRY'S OFFICE—HALLWAY—CONTINUOUS DAY (ONE)

Larry walks past the transgender bathroom (half man-half woman sign displayed on door) and pauses. He looks both ways down the hallway to see if anyone else is in the hall. He grabs the door handle and it's locked. He sighs and continues to the next door/the regular bathroom.

8. INT. BATHROOM—WALKING IN—CONTINUOUS DAY (ONE)

Larry walks into the bathroom and opens a stall door. He notices the previous user didn't flush the toilet he is about to use. Larry (over)reacts and stumbles back/away from the stall. As Larry is backing away, a man enters the bathroom. The man sees Larry backing away from the stall and looks in thru the stall door. He sees the unflushed toilet and yells at Larry, "Ugghh. Did you leave *THAT* in there? Asshole!" Larry tries to explain that it wasn't him but the man storms out. Larry leaves the bathroom.

9. INT. LARRY'S OFFICE—HALLWAY—CONTINUOUS DAY (ONE)

Larry walks up to **ANTOINETTE's** desk and asks her for the transgender bathroom key. She asks why he wants it. Larry explains that no one uses it and it's much cleaner.

Larry: "It's like having my own private bathroom."

Antoinette says that she lent the key to DINO from Big Dog productions. Larry corrects Antoinette, "Dog."

Antoinette: "Oh yeah, he likes to be called 'Dog'. He's actually in his office now if you want to ask him for the key."

Larry thanks Antoinette and walks to Dog's office. He approaches Dog's office and sees a "beware of dog!" sign on the door. Larry rolls his eyes. Snoring (audio dub) is heard coming from Dog's office. Larry slowly opens Dog's door.

10. INT. DOG'S OFFICE—DOORWAY/IN OFFICE— CONTINUOUS DAY (ONE)

Larry sticks his head into the office and sees **DOG** is sleeping at his desk. Larry is about to leave but notices the bathroom key on the desk underneath Dog's arm. Larry quietly makes his way toward Dog's desk. Larry slowly reaches out for the key and grabs it. The key is 'stuck' underneath Dog's arm. Larry gently pushes and pulls at the key trying to retrieve it. Dog's begins to stir. Larry pauses and tries to remove the key. He retrieves the key and 'backs' his way out of Dog's office.

11. INT. LARRY'S OFFICE—HALLWAY—CONTINUOUS DAY (ONE)

Larry is approaching the transgender bathroom with the key in his hand and comes face-to face with **CAITLYN JENNER** exiting the transgender bathroom. Larry and Caitlyn briefly chat/make small talk. In the midst of chatting, Larry starts talking about running and how he tries to run for exercise whenever he's not tired. He asks Caitlyn about Bruce's Olympic titles and gold medals. Caitlyn reacts as if she doesn't know what Larry's talking about.

Larry (frustrated): "I don't get why you can't discuss some of your accomplishments as Bruce...it's still you...YOU won the gold medals, YOU set those records, it was all YOU."

Caitlyn: "That was a different me."

Larry: "A different you? Then let me talk to Bruce. Can I talk to Bruce for a second? Put Bruce on the line."

Caitlyn is noticeably offended. Larry does the 'Lie-Eye-Stare' with Caitlyn while asking "is 'Bruce' still in there?". Caitlyn tells Larry she's offended and upset by his behavior. Larry apologizes. Caitlyn observes the key in Larry's hand and asks Larry where he's heading. Larry says he's going to the restroom. Larry admits to using the transgender restroom because it's cleaner and because "nobody uses it."

Caitlyn: "Nobody?"

Larry and Caitlyn argue over the use of the bathroom.

Larry (side)steps around Caitlyn, unlocks the bathroom door and (as he steps inside) and remarks:

Larry: "If you run into Bruce, tell HIM I said 'hello'."

12. INT. LARRY'S HOUSE – KITCHEN—NIGHT (TWO)
LEON is standing in the kitchen, making a sandwich. Larry walks in and sees a bag of Cheetos spilled on the counter. Larry asks Leon about the mess. Leon puts a handful of Cheetos on his sandwich and closes it. He holds up the sandwich.

Leon: "THAT'S a fuckin' sandwich."

Larry: "Hmm, 'a fuckin' sandwich', I don't think I've ever had one of those. I've had a regular sandwich before, but never a 'fuckin' sandwich'. You know, I gotta try it sometime, 'a fuckin' sandwich'."

Leon offers Larry a bite from his half-eaten sandwich. Larry declines.

Larry: "Hey, let me ask you something. The other day there was this cute black woman at this restaurant and..."

Leon (interrupting): "Whoa!! Larry, my man!" (while sucking the Cheeto residue off his fingers).

Leon slaps Larry on his arm. Larry looks down where Leon touched his jacket to see if there is a stain from Leon's Cheeto 'fingers'.

Leon: "So what happened? Did you do your *dizzle*?"

Larry: "No, I tried to talk to her but she seemed... uninterested."

Larry continues explaining how his 'moves' don't work on black women.

Leon: "Yeah, you're right, if you want a taste of chocolate, you gotta cut the Mr. Rogers shit."

Leon makes fun of the way Larry dresses and offers Larry some advice. Leon gives Larry pointers on how to dress to impress a black woman. After a bit of discussion, Leon tells Larry that he should wear his pants a little lower and walk with a rhythm to his step. Larry laughs and disagrees with Leon's advice.

13. EXT. COFFEE SHOP - OUTSIDE SEATING AREA - DAY (TWO)

Larry is finishing lunch with **TED** and **MARY**. They talk about Susie's birthday and the gifts they're giving her. Larry says he hasn't decided what to get her and that he'll probably pick up a bottle of wine on his way to the party. They pay their lunch bill and leave.

14. INT. LARRY'S CAR – DRIVING - DAY (TWO)

Larry is driving home from the restaurant. As he makes a phone call, a pickup truck cuts him off. Larry honks his horn, opens his window, and starts yelling. The man sticks his head out the window of his truck, looks back at Larry, and shouts "Asshole!". Larry notices a "How's my driving?" sticker on the back of the man's truck. He dials the phone number printed on the "How's my driving?" bumper sticker. The call goes into automated voicemail. Larry leaves an angry voicemail about the man who just cut him off, calling him a "schmohawk" and criticizing his driving.

15. INT. JEFF'S HOUSE - LIVING ROOM - NIGHT (TWO)

SUSIE is seated behind a table stacked with gifts. Larry, Jeff, Ted, Mary, **SAMMI** and a group of other people are watching Susie open the gifts. As Susie is handed each gift, she opens a card and reads who it's from. Larry is telling Jeff about his encounter with Caitlyn Jenner. Susie stands up and clangs a spoon against a wine glass to get the attention of the room. She tells everyone that the card she's holding is from Sammi and reads it out loud. The card ends with, "World's Greatest Mom!". Susie opens the gift bag from Sammi and it's a coffee mug that says, "WORLD'S GREATEST MOM!" Everyone applauds. Larry turns to Jeff and says, "World's Greatest? That's a bit much, don't you think?" Larry and Jeff joke about the "World's Greatest" phrase and how it's overused and hacky. Larry mockingly says, "Oooh, the world's greatest burger, the world's greatest coffee, (etc.)..." Jeff picks up a slice of cake and (mocking) says, "It's the world's greatest. Want a piece?"

16. INT. GROCERY STORE - AISLE – DAY (THREE)

Larry is walking past the aisles of a grocery store and sees the attractive black woman from the restaurant. Larry hides in an adjacent aisle. He recalls what Leon told him. (Audio Dub: Leon's advice to Larry on how to impress a black woman). Larry lowers his pants a bit and walks into her aisle. He walks past her slightly bobbing back and forth. He stops right next to her and picks up something off the shelf. He looks over at what she's holding and recommends a different product. She smiles at Larry, recognizes him from the restaurant and say's 'hello'. She notices Larry's pants are pulled down low. She questions Larry about the sagging pants. Larry lies and says that he forgot to wear a belt. She laughs and smiles. Larry pulls up his pants. She asks Larry about the bag of Cheetos that he's holding. He tells her they're for medical research. Larry asks her out for coffee. She says, "you're funny, okay. What's your name?" Larry gives her his name and asks for hers. She says, "Mercedes." Larry jokes, "hmm, 'Mercedes'. Like the car?" Larry says "good thing your parents didn't like BUICK." She laughs and hands her phone to Larry so he can type his number in. Larry types in his number and hands the phone back to her. She says, "I'll call you later", smiles, and walks away.

17. INT. LARRY'S HOUSE – KITCHEN - DAY (THREE)

Larry is putting groceries away and tells Leon what happened at the grocery store. Larry explains that he tried to sag his pants a little bit but it didn't work. Leon starts giving him more inappropriate advice and asks Larry, "Hey, did you get my shit?" Larry throws a bag of Cheetos at Leon and he catches it. Leon looks at the bag and says, "Oh yeah! Thanks Larry!" Larry continues putting the groceries away.

18. EXT. COFFEE SHOP—SIDEWALK—DAY (THREE)
Larry is approaching a coffee shop and sees a sign that says, "World's Greatest Coffee!" Larry sighs and shakes his head. He enters the coffee shop.

19. INT. COFFEE SHOP –IN LINE—CONTINUOUS – DAY (THREE)
Larry walks up to the **CASHIER** and orders a coffee and a cookie. Larry pays for his order and steps aside to wait for his coffee. The barista hands Larry his cookie. He takes it and steps back to wait for his coffee.

20. EXT. COFFEE SHOP—PARKING LOT – CONTINUOUS-DAY (THREE)
The pickup truck that cut off Larry earlier parks next to Larry's car. The (same) driver (from scene 14) gets out of his truck. He walks past Larry's Prius and stops. He stares at Larry's car, and looks into the coffee shop. He sees Larry through the coffee shop window. He looks back and forth between Larry and his Prius. He recognizes Larry and the Prius. The man walks back to his truck, grabs a large envelope from inside and walks to the back of Larry's car. He kneels down behind Larry's Prius.

21. INT. COFFEE SHOP – DRINK COUNTER - CONTINUOUS - DAY (THREE)
While Larry is waiting for his coffee, he sees the handicap

man's caretaker (from scene 5) waiting for coffee. Larry says hello and tries to apologize. The caretaker tells Larry how disturbing the restaurant situation was and that Larry should be ashamed. Larry is fed up with the caretaker blaming him.

Larry: "You know what? If you don't believe me, fine, but I didn't write those words, I was typing out whatever he told me to because he couldn't text it himself, and by the way, WHERE were you during all of this? You're the 'caretaker', you're supposed to be the one helping him, not me, asshole."

Larry begins to eat the cookie. The cashier yells out "David!" to let Larry know his coffee is ready. While carrying the cookie in one hand, he grabs his coffee with the other. As Larry picks up the coffee, his phone rings in his (upper) coat pocket. Larry looks down at his phone and up at the caretaker. Larry shrugs and smiles and motions/nods with his head (expecting the caretaker to answer the phone for him). The caretaker calls Larry a "asshole" and walks away. Larry's phone continues to ring.

22. EXT. COFFEE SHOP – LARRY'S CAR—CONTINUOUS — DAY (THREE)

Larry finishes the cookie, walks to his car and gets in. He backs out of the spot to leave (camera shot at front of car). As he drives away, (camera shot at rear of car) a "WORLD'S GREATEST ASSHOLE!" sticker is seen on Larry's rear bumper.

FADE OUT/Cue Music.

(END)

16

BLACK Tie Optional

Even before we (Ray and John) considered leaving the corporate rat race, we were noticing comic 'opportunities'. One memorable incident started with an overheard rude comment from a colleague to another colleague in the office break room: "You no wear white after Labor Day". No, that's not a grammatical mistake, that's exactly how it was uttered. The reply was unintelligible. A meaningless exchange until you add in these factors: Both people were Asian. The one making the comment did not have a good command of the English language and routinely wore nothing but black clothes. The other one always wore white clothes, and to put it impolitely, was privately referred to as "Mushmouth". Not only was it a strain to understand one fourth of what she said, her writing style was equally atrocious. And yet they were militant when it came to equal opportunity and (trying to) fit in with the rest of the staff. We talked it over as a possible episode idea but dismissed it – "Not enough there". But the theme kept popping up.

As Thanksgiving approached that year, our favorite coffee shop in LA closed. It was an addictive little place – quiet, done in black decor with white tablecloths, excellent espresso, and an incredibly cute server named Helena. The owner however, had a moody personality---we called him KILLER---and Ray suggested we give him a gift of a mood ring so that we could tell if he was having an up or down day. After operating as a coffee shop for less than a year, KILLER decided to go in a different direction. A few weeks later, it re-opened as a burger joint. The change was not a welcome one. The décor was simple: WHITE. The walls, the lights, the tables, the plates, the signage, even the servers --- ALL WHITE. Times change, but we never went back.

The approach of Thanksgiving also meant the family dinners were near. We kicked around a few ideas about a

Thanksgiving dinner episode and that's when we hit on the episode's central theme: BLACK and WHITE. It wasn't just common to Thanksgiving, it WAS Thanksgiving. From arguments over white meat and dark meat to BLACK Friday shopping. Once we started compiling a list, we couldn't stop. White rice. White Potatoes, White Wine, Barry White ("......wait, he's BLACK!").

Back at the office, an invitation (e-mail) to the company Christmas party had been sent out by "Mushmouth". We had to decode the message using a crystal ball. Apparently, there would be a party held on (an unspecified) Tuesday evening at a dumpy bar near the office (no address listed). Spouses were "no invited" and "Participate employees contribute $10 charge cover". The last line clinched it: "Business dress prescribed. Black-Tie Optional". Did the moron that wrote this even know what Black-Tie meant? For CHRIST'S SAKE, 'casual' attire at the office had already sunk to pajama bottoms and dirty flannel shirts. Who in their right mind would change into black-tie attire?

Back in the present, we continued to make progress with the Curb Your Enthusiasm production company. As we noted in Chapter 14, we were seeing the light at the end of the tunnel. An Executive Producer associated with Curb Your Enthusiasm wanted to talk with us. Although the Producer initially wouldn't tell us what the discussion was to be about, it turned out for the best. The next step was meeting the rest of the Curb Your Enthusiasm Production company. Arrangements were made, first class seats were booked, and before we knew it, we were in OUR trailer on the location set of Curb Your Enthusiasm, waiting for an audience with THE KING (Larry David).

No longer was our adventure a break-even (or losing) proposition. We were:

17

Episode 8

"*Back* in BLACK"

Synopsis: Larry and Lewis are 'suffering' from the effects of aging and start down different paths towards revitalization.

Scenes: 15

Cast: Larry, Ricard Lewis, Jeff, Susie, Leon, two supermodel type women, various women (dates) for Larry.

Special Guest: Ron Popeil as THE CART VENDOR.

"*Back* in BLACK"

1. EXT. FRONT OF MEDICAL BUILDING – DAY (ONE)

LARRY is exiting a medical office building walking with a slight limp, holding his backside with one hand, and heading towards his car. **LEON** is driving Larry's car, parked in front of the building. Larry opens the passenger door and slowly sits down.

Leon: "Why I pickin' you up, LD?"

Larry: "I had an exam and didn't feel up to driving."

Leon: "An exam? Like a driver's test?"

Larry: "No. A digital exam."

Leon: "Digital? Is that, like, with computers?"

Larry: "No. DIGITAL!...like with fingers. I think that Doctor shoved his entire fist in my tuchus."

Leon: "Tuchus? You let someone put his hands IN your ass?...and you PAID him to do this...this Gluttonous-Maximus job???"

Larry: "Yeah...Gluttonous-Maximus."

Leon: "You gettin' old, LD."

Larry: "Yeah...old...and tired."

Leon: "You need a pick-me-up. Let's go for spicy Thai food."

Larry: "Thai? My ass is already on fire. Uggghh...I'm supposed to meet Lewis. Head east...you can drop me off in Brentwood."

2. INT. RESTAURANT - DAY (ONE)
RICHARD LEWIS and Larry are sitting at a table eating lunch. Richard gripes about the lack of work he's been getting lately --- that he isn't getting any callbacks and every deal he put together and pitched last month was rejected. Larry ignores Lewis' griping and talks of feeling tired and sluggish. Lewis ignores Larry's griping and continues to complain about his lack of opportunities and thinks it might be age discrimination. Larry ignores Lewis' griping.

Larry: "Discrimination? I've got problems of my own. I just had someone's arm up my backside for 10 minutes and it cost me $300, and there was no happy ending."

Lewis: "You're just getting OLD, Larry. We're all getting older, but what do 'I' do? I still need the work."

Larry: "Maybe the all-black thing isn't working for you anymore. WHY do you wear all black? It's too depressing. Maybe you need to spice it up? Let's wrap this up. I need to meet Jeff at Grand Central Market and Leon is picking me up in ten minutes."

The **SERVER** arrives and Larry asks for the bill. The server pulls it from her apron pocket, looks at Larry, and tells him 'I'll just go apply the senior discount and bring this right back' and leaves.

3. EXT. SIDEWALK IN FRONT OF GRAND CENTRAL MARKET - DAY (ONE)

JEFF is talking to a **CART VENDOR** (**Ron Popeil**) in front of Grand Central Market as Larry and Leon walk up. Leon spots two **SUPER-MODEL** type **WOMEN**, tells Larry he'll 'catch up' with him later and heads toward the women.

Jeff (to Larry): "Larry--over here."

Larry (to Jeff): "Let's go inside and get some coffee. I need to sit down"

Jeff (to Larry): "Jesus, Larry, you look terrible."

Larry ('barking'): "INSIDE. COFFEE. SIT. NOW!"

Jeff (to Larry): "OK, OK...geez, what crawled up your backside and died?"

Larry: "A $1500 an hour doctor."

Jeff: "A WHAT?"

Cart Vendor (to Larry): "Sir, may I offer you some help?"

Larry: "You got coffee?"

Cart Vendor (to Larry): "No. Your friend is right. You don't look well. And you sound tired..."

Larry: "Thanks, Doc. Did you buy your medical degree from another cart vendor?"

Cart Vendor (to Larry): "No. But I would recommend

THIS." (Vendor holds up a black wire mesh bracelet). "Its real name is very hard to pronounce. It comes from Seychelles. I call it, *THE MAGIC BRACELET*. It has powers— it will make you more energetic, you'll be more active, better rested, and you'll just feel more youthful."

Larry: "Seychelles? Sure, sure...and it probably makes julienne fries too, right?"

Leon (smiling broadly) approaches Larry, Jeff and the vendor with the two young supermodel women (one on each arm).

Cart Vendor (to Larry): "I wear one...but don't take my word for it. Look, mister, I'm eighty years old and these are my girlfriends."

The two super models both leave Leon's side and place their arms around the cart vendor. Leon's smile fades.

Leon: "I lost my DIZZLE."

Super-models (in unison, to cart vendor): "Come on Ronny, you promised take us roller blading on the Venice boardwalk."

Larry: "You take credit cards?"

Jeff: "What's with this necklace? *Magic*, too?"

Cart Vendor (to Jeff): "No, I call that one THE PREDICTOR. It changes color depending on the mood of the person wearing it. Red means angry. Blue means relaxed, Gold means happy, and Black means, ummmm,

Black means excited (the cart vendor looks at Leon)...he GETS IT...'excited'." (The cart vendor brushes back the long blond hair of one of the supermodels to reveal the necklace shining black) "...EX-CITED, if ya know what I mean."

Jeff: "SOLD. Put it on his (gesturing towards Larry) bill."

Cart Vendor: "Here you are (the vendor hands Jeff and Larry small boxes and note cards). It comes with a special care and handling card –it's important---DON'T let the bracelet get wet---no swimming, no showering--it'll turn gray and lose all its power. And the pendent--don't let the pendent get cold—it has to stay above 50 degrees. If it gets below 50, it'll turn black permanently. Make sure you read these cards—you don't want to ruin the items."

4. INT./EXT. VARIOUS – DAY (TWO)
Fast/Slide-cut collage scenes* (Larry has RENEWED energy):
-Larry jogging with an attractive woman.
-Larry playing racquetball with a (different) attractive woman.
-Larry looking in bathroom mirror at what appears to be new hair on his head.
-Larry's vision improves (printed words come into focus without wearing his glasses).
-Larry working out in an all-women Zumba class.
-Larry in bed with the Zumba instructor.

*All scenes feature shot of the bracelet on Larry's wrist.

5. INT. JEFF'S HOUSE – DAY (THREE)
Jeff has given Susie the pendant. **SUSIE** is wearing it around her neck, just above her cleavage and is showing it to Larry. Larry looks at it and notices the color:

Larry: "What an unusual piece—and the color of the stone---is that gold?...you seem VERY happy with it."

Larry looks at Jeff and winks.

Susie: "It's very exotic. It reflects the light in unusual ways."

Larry looks at the pendant for an 'uncomfortable' length of time. Susie accuses Larry of staring at her breasts and demands Larry get out.

6. INT. SALON – DAY (FOUR)
Lewis is in a salon being attended to by a stylist. Lewis is wearing stylish, all white clothing. He's on the phone with Larry telling him he's completely changed his look –it's the 'NEW-AGE' LEWIS. Lewis (enthusiastically) tells Larry he has several pitch meetings lined up. (Lewis ends the call.)

7. INT. LARRY'S HOUSE – NIGHT (FOUR)
Larry is hosting party at his house. Several guest are already there/standing in the living room. Another guest arrives (doorbell heard) and Larry answers the door. A **WOMAN GUEST** enters and hands Larry a platter of hors d'oeuvres.

WOMAN GUEST: "Larry. HERE. It's an oyster, liver, goat cheese torta...and you KNOW what oysters are good for...?"

The Woman Guest walks to a group of other guests and leaves Larry alone holding the platter. Larry looks at the appetizer, sniffs it and pulls it away from his face. Larry turns to another (male) guest and offers him an appetizer.

Larry: "It's oysters. And Liver. And cheese. And...torta."

The guest takes an appetizer and places it in his mouth. His face contorts and he (immediately) spits the appetizer into a napkin, wads it up, places the balled up napkin in Larry's hand and says, 'No, thanks.'

Larry turns and hands the platter to Jeff.

Larry: "It's oysters-cheese-torta things....and you KNOW what oysters are good for...I'll be right back—I have to wash my hands."

< SCENE TRANSITION >

Larry enters the kitchen and approaches the sink. The sink is equipped with a touchless faucet that turns on the water flow without touching a handle. Larry moves his hands under the faucet and nothing happens. He tries again without success. Larry moves his hands directly against the sensor on the faucet and the water trickles out, but stops before Larry can get his hands under the water flow. Larry repeats several times without success. Larry moves his hands under the faucet and moves them in a wild-exaggerated manner. The water starts flowing at full volume spraying Larry's hands and wrists, soaking the bracelet. Larry doesn't realize water has soaked the bracelet and dries his hands.

< SCENE TRANSITION >

Larry returns to the living room. Jeff is holding the platter and feeding oyster appetizers to Susie. Jeff is watching the pendant hanging from Susie's neck. Its color shifts from gold to black. Jeff (discreetly) checks the color description card that came with the pendant. Jeff looks at the pendant again, places his hand on Susie's neck and (abruptly) tells Larry, 'We're leaving'.

8. EXT. JEFF'S CAR – NIGHT (FOUR)
Jeff and Susie are in the car driving away from Larry's house. Susie is stroking Jeff's hair. The pendant can be seen shimmering in black. Susie suggests they stop and pick up a quart of the new 'dragon's breath' nitrogen ice cream to have 'afterward'.

Jeff (smiling): "Let's get two!"

9. INT. JEFF'S HOUSE – NIGHT (FOUR)
Jeff and Susie are in the kitchen wearing robes and eating ice cream. Susie is complimenting Jeff on his 'performance'. Jeff looks at Susie's pendent (showing blue) and (discreetly) checks the description card (blue=relaxed) and smiles. Jeff says he's going to have another scoop of the ice cream and walks to the freezer. Susie leans forward reaching for a napkin. As she leans forward the pendant swings forwards and dips into her bowl of ice cream. Susie curses and wipes the pendant clean. Jeff returns from the freezer (not seeing the pendant falling into the ice cream). As Jeff places the ice cream on the counter, he observes the pendant has changed from blue to black.
Jeff smiles and turns to Susie

Jeff: "Maybe I'll skip the second round of ice cream..."

10. INT. LARRY'S HOUSE – DAY (FIVE)
Larry is tired and sluggish. He is wearing the bracelet and it has turned gray. The phone rings. (Caller ID shows Richard

Lewis.) Larry answers. Lewis gripes about not getting any offers because of his NEW look --- the WHITE look Larry suggested isn't working and he isn't getting any callbacks. Every deal he put together and pitched was rejected, and the only offer he received was to do a promo for the White House/Black Market chain. Larry blows him off with 'I have problems of my own'. Larry, noticing the bracelet has turned gray, pulls out the care card and realizes the bracelet is ruined. Larry (abruptly) ends the call.

11. INT. SALON – DAY (SIX)
Lewis is in a salon being attended to by a stylist. Lewis is wearing all black. He's on the phone with Larry telling him he's completely changed his look.

Lewis: "I'm back in BLACK, Larry. Producers and directors wanted my black look all along. Can't talk---too busy." (Lewis abruptly ends the call).

12. EXT. GRAND CENTRAL MARKET– DAY (SIX)
Larry returns to Grand Central market and finds the vendor packing up.

Larry: "I need a new bracelet."

Cart Vendor: "...JUST sold the last bracelet--no more available...but I do have this ring..."

Larry: "A ring? I don't like wearing rings on my fingers"

Cart Vendor: "mmmmm, no, it's not that kind of ring."

Larry: "Earring???"

Cart Vendor: "No. It's a nipple ring."

Larry: "Me? A nipple ring? I don't think so."

Larry leaves (shuffling/dragging his feet).

13. INT./EXT. VARIOUS – DAY (FIVE)
Fast/Slide-cut collage scenes (Larry still sluggish and tired):
-Larry shuffling along a trail as attractive woman jog past him.
-Larry shuffles up to a (glass wall) racquetball court and pauses to look in, watching two attractive woman play.
-Larry looking in bathroom mirror, holding hair in his hands that is coming out of his head.
-Larry's vision deteriorates (printed words are fuzzy) and Larry (wearing his glasses) is holding a magazine with an outstretched arm.
-Larry slowly shuffles past the Zumba class/building, looks in thru the window and sees the Zumba instructor, who waves him in. Larry continues down the sidewalk, dragging his feet.

14. INT. JEFF'S HOUSE – DAY (SIX)
Jeff is looking at Susie and sees the pendant glowing black. Jeff (discreetly) checks the mood indicator card (Black =excited). Jeff presumes Susie is 'excited'. He walks up behind Susie and squeezes her backside. Susie turns and hits Jeff and shouts at him, 'WHAT the FUCK?'.

15. EXT. JOGGING PATH – DAY (SIX)
Larry is jogging (energetic/smiling) with the Zumba instructor. Larry is wearing a tight t-shirt. A nipple ring outline can be seen thru Larry's shirt.

FADE OUT/Cue Music.

(END)

18

The **G**ift of **G**ab

"We can't make this stuff up." We said it over and over. The reality of our situations was just *too* **G**ood.

We rapidly realized a significant part of this business is networking. Ray is particularly good chatting up the right people, but since we are a writing team, John was obligated to go along for the ride. One of our early lessons was being/acting smart is not the same as being right or doing the right thing.

During our search for an Agent (more on that can be found in Chapter 6), we were introduced to Geoff. That's Geoff WITH A '**G**' as Geoff would tell every single person he encountered (as though Jeff with a 'J' was something less). We also would find out that Geoff (WITH A '**G**') was somewhat obsessed with the letter '**G**'. We made note of it and may have forgotten about him if not for another of Geoff's peculiarities. He insisted on meeting us for a round of golf--not terribly unusual for LA--and then proceeded to cheat on every single hole. Geoff seemed to think the rules of golf allowed him to kick his ball into an improved position, whether on the fairway or the green. Geoff may have shot a 92, but he KICKED an additional 18. And this is someone we are going to trust to represent us? We **G**ave **G**eoff a **G**iant **G**oodbye.

Another networking event involved a musician. It quickly became obvious this person was, in polite terms, a 'favor-mooch' (or, to borrow from Larry David: "You can't make an empty gesture without this person taking advantage of it.").

The favor-mooch idea had been used, but this individual accidentally provided a new twist. He had been to the eye doctor earlier in the day and was 'working the crowd' at a party to get (mooch) a ride home as his eyes had been dilated at the doctor. As he moved about the room, his impaired vision (seemingly) was causing problems with depth perception and precision. He reached out to greet a woman and accidentally shook her breast instead of her hand. He attempted to place his drink on a counter and dropped it on the floor. *THIS* was an idea we could use.

The final piece of the puzzle came in the form of an acquaintance of Ray's--another musician. In search of networking possibilities, Ray had been to a number of Kenny G concerts and had met him on several occasions. We tossed around a few ideas and Ray presented the concept to Kenny G. Kenny was receptive (and amused), so we pulled our ideas together and found...

19

Episode 9

"The 'G' Spot"

Synopsis: Larry attempts to impress his girlfriend by arranging a private concert for her by Kenny G...but Larry's unfortunate quest for the truth and inability to let go leads to utter destruction.

Scenes: 15

Cast: Larry, Larry's girlfriend Rita, Leon, Jeff, Jeff's cousin-Geoff; Restaurant Waiter, Jeff's admin assistant, Plumber, Golf course starter, Art gallery patrons.

Special Guest: Kenny G as himself.

"The 'G' Spot"

1. INT. ART GALLERY SHOWROOM – NIGHT (ONE)
Scene opens with a close-up of a Georgia O'Keeffe-esque painting of a vagina. **LARRY** and his girlfriend, **RITA** are both admiring her painting on the wall in her art gallery. The gallery is full of vagina paintings and sculptures of all shapes and sizes. Rita explains her art piece.

Rita: "I call it, 'Morning Dew'."

Larry teases Rita about the art in her gallery.

Larry: "Why give it a name? Just call it, Vagina1, Vagina2 …they're all vaginas, what's the difference? And you know what?…Not all vaginas are beautiful."

Rita argues the point.

Rita: "They're all unique and all different, like snowflakes. That's why ALL my art consists of them."

Larry laughs at her snowflake-vagina analogy. Rita turns off the lights and prepares to leave. Larry gestures towards the door, "Ready for dinner?" Rita locks the doors and says she's starving. Larry and Rita leave.

2. INT. RESTAURANT – SITTING AT TABLE – LATER - NIGHT (ONE)
Larry and Rita are finishing dinner. Larry mentions that he would like to get Rita something special for her birthday. Rita objects.

Rita: "Larry, that's sweet, but honestly, I don't need anything. I have everything I need right here."

Larry looks around confused. Rita puts her hand on Larry's.

Rita: "YOU. You're everything I need Larry."

Larry: "ME? You must not need too much then, huh? Come on, there must be something? Isn't there anything you've ever wanted and never received for your birthday?"

Rita (nervous-embarrassed laugh) scratches the back of her head.

Rita: "Well, there's this one thing...oh my God, I can't believe I'm telling you this."

Larry: "What? What is it?"

Rita (embarrassed): "Ever since I was a teenager, I've had a crush on this one jazz artist. I love the way he plays the notes...just everything about him. I used to dream about meeting him and having my own private concert."

Larry (interrupting): "Okay, who is this 'jazz artist'?"

Rita: "It's kind of funny, you might know him, it's...Kenny G."

Larry (abruptly): "Why would you assume I know him?"

Rita (defensive): "I don't know. You know...a lot of people know him and..."

Larry (interrupting): "Say it. Go ahead. It's because we're 'fellow' Jews? You know, Jews don't have that whole 'brotherhood' thing. We're a different breed."

Rita (excited): "So you DO know him?"

Larry: "Eh. I know him but I don't KNOW him. I'll see what I can do."

Rita: "If you can make that happen, I would be very grateful. That would be the best gift I've ever received Larry! And who knows, maybe I'll give you *a gift* in return."

The **WAITER** comes over with a slice of cake with a candle in it. He is accompanied by a group of other staff members. The waiter (enthusiastically) says, "I couldn't help overhearing that it was someone's birthday at this table. Who's celebrating?" Larry looks over at Rita. She raises her hand and says, "Guilty." The waiter says, "Well, congratulations! Happy Birthday!" He sets down two forks and a slice of cake with a candle in it. The waiter and staff members all begin singing Happy Birthday. Rita is smiling and singing along. Larry has a look of disgust and pain on his face as he refuses to participate in singing the birthday song. They finish the song and disperse. Rita blows out the candle. Larry rants to Rita about how he thinks it's 'lame' when restaurants do the Happy Birthday song.

Rita: "Look on the bright side, free desert!"

Larry agrees and picks up a fork. He is about to take a bite of the cake and notices a piece of lettuce stuck to his fork. He puts the dirty fork back down on the table and looks around for an extra place setting. He sees a non-occupied table and walks over to it. Larry takes a place setting off the empty table and walks back to his seat. As he is about to sit down, the waiter rushes over.

Waiter: "Sir, what do you think you're doing?"

Larry looks around, confused as to who the waiter is speaking to.

Larry: "What?"

Waiter (loudly): "You walked over to that table and stole a place setting."

Larry (gesturing with his fork): "Did I steal a place setting? No. Did I replace a dirty fork? Yes, yes I did."

Waiter: "What?"

Larry picks up the dirty fork and holds it up (close) to the waiter's face. There is a noticeable piece of lettuce stuck to it.

Waiter: "You can't just walk over and steal someone's silverware!"

Larry: "Someone's?? No one was sitting there, YOU gave me a dirty fork. I needed a clean fork, I got a clean fork...and what's with you accusing me of stealing? Did I put the fork in my jacket and walk out of the restaurant? No. The fork has not left the building, therefore, I did NOT steal anything."

Waiter (yelling): "Well, maybe you didn't steal it from the establishment, but you took it right out of the hands of another customer."

Larry: "Look, I know what stealing a fork is and this was not it. I don't have to explain myself!"

Larry asks for the bill. The waiter calls Larry a "fork thief" and briefly leaves to get Larry his check. Larry holds up the fork and smiles. The waiter hands Larry his check and walks away. Larry opens it up and sees that the waiter charged him for the dessert. Larry calls the waiter back and begins to question the charge for the dessert.

Waiter (formal/unfriendly): "Problem?"

Larry accuses the waiter of charging him for the 'free' birthday dessert.

Larry (arguing): "THIS, is stealing! You know what? I'm going to 'steal' the price of the cake out of your tip!"

Waiter (walking away from the table): "A tip? Here's a TIP: don't steal silverware!"

Larry (yells back): "Ya know what?...Go FORK yourself."
Larry is seen crossing out the original tip and writing in a smaller amount.

3. INT. JEFF'S OFFICE BUILDING – OFFICE AREA/RESTROOM – DAY (TWO)

Larry enters an office and is greeted by an **ADMIN** seated behind a desk.

Admin: "Hello Mr. David. Jeff can see you now."

Larry: "Give me a minute...I'm going to use the restroom first."

< SCENE TRANSITION >

Larry walks into a bathroom stall. He begins to remove a paper seat cover from the dispenser and it rips. Larry shakes his head and tries again. He almost gets another cover out and it rips again. Larry (frustrated) tries a third time and pulls the seat cover out the dispenser very slowly. The cover comes out intact. Larry, holding the paper seat cover, carefully places it on the seat. He turns, unbuckles his belt and is about to sit down when the automatic flush sensor triggers and sucks the paper cover into the toilet. Larry looks behind him and sees that the cover is gone. He reaches over to take another paper cover and it rips. Once again, he slowly pulls out a complete seat cover and carefully sets it down on the toilet. Larry turns and (very slowly) begins squatting down on the toilet, trying not to trip the sensor. As Larry is nearly seated, the sensor triggers the seat cover is again sucked away. Larry angrily grunts and forcefully grabs a handful of seat covers out of the box all at once (1.5" thick). He slaps the thick stack of seat covers on the toilet seat. The auto flush activates. Larry turns to see the thick stack of seat covers flutter but stay put as the auto flush vacuum attempts to pull the thick stack into the bowl. Larry forcefully sits down on the toilet.

4. INT. JEFF'S OFFICE BUILDING – JEFF'S OFFICE – DAY (TWO)

Larry, out of breath and angry, walks into Jeff's office. **JEFF** asks Larry, "What's wrong with you?" Larry explains what happened in the bathroom with the toilet seat covers and the flush sensor. Jeff laughs and says that's why he uses the bathrooms on the second floor because they don't have the sensors. Larry tells Jeff about Rita's birthday wish.

Larry: "How am I supposed to get Kenny G, let alone a private show."

Jeff (excited): "Okay, you're not going to believe this. My cousin, you know, big music guy..."

Larry (interrupting): "Your cousin Geoff?"

Jeff: "Yeah, Geoff! With a 'G'. He's going to be in town this week. I'm going golfing with him this Sunday. Guess who he represents?"

Larry (excited): "Kenny G?!"

Jeff: "No... but guess who the guy he represents is friends with?"

Larry (irritated): "Who?"

Jeff: "Kenny fucking G! And get this, he's a huge golfer. Huge!"

Larry: "Do you think you can get Kenny to come with you this Sunday?"

Jeff: "I don't see why not. I'll see what I can do. If Kenny can make it, I'll squeeze you in the foursome. You can ask him about the private show yourself."

Larry (smiling): "What are the odds?"

[176]

Jeff (jokingly): "1 in 46."

5. INT. LARRY'S HOUSE – KITCHEN – DAY (THREE)
LEON is eating cereal straight out of the box. Larry complains that Leon eats all his food.

Larry: "You act like you own the place. You eat my food, you wear my clothes, you use my bathroom!"

Leon: "I don't wear your baggy ass clothes, walking around like Mr. Rogers and shit. And, I told you to get my toilet fixed Larry. That shit don't work. The water doesn't go down, it just sprays straight up my asshole, Larry. It's like trying to take a shit in a water fountain."

Larry: "Why would you take a shit in a water fountain?"

Leon: "Of course I wouldn't shit in a water fountain, I was givin' an analogy, vis-à-vis, of what it feels like to shit in that broken-ass toilet."

Larry (confused): "Vis-à-vis??"

Leon: "Vis-à-vis."

Larry: Vis-à-vis. Fair enough. I'll call someone to fix it tomorrow."

Leon asks Larry about his attire. Larry is in his golfing clothes. He explains that he is going golfing with Jeff and Kenny G.

Larry: "I'm going ask Kenny G if he'd play a private show for Rita."

Leon: "Ahhh shit! The G!"

Larry: "You know Kenny G?"
Leon: "Fuck yeah, I know Kenny G, that guy *DESTROYS the pussy!*"

Larry looks at Leon with a puzzled expression.

Larry: *"Destroys the pussy?"*

Leon: "Yeah, destroys the pussy! That guy gets bitches left and right!"

Larry jokes about the pussy destroyer comment.

Larry: "Hmm, 'Kenny G *destroys pussy*'...good to know."

Leon walks out of the kitchen and yells back.

Leon: "I DO live here Larry! LB and LD, we in this shit together!"

6. INT. GOLF COURSE CLUBHOUSE – TABLE – DAY (THREE)

Larry and Jeff walk into the clubhouse and give their names to the golf course **STARTER**. He can't find either of them on the list. Jeff and Larry look at each other and shrug. Jeff insists that the starter check again, but this time, "Try Geoff, with a 'G'." Jeff looks at Larry and shakes his head. No tee reservations are found. Larry and Jeff step aside to wait for **KENNY G** and **GEOFF** (Jeff's cousin) to arrive. Kenny and Geoff arrive and introduce themselves. Kenny walks up to the starter.

Kenny G: "G, party of four."

The starter points out the location of the first tee and says, "Ahh, right this way Mr. G." They get in their carts and drive off.

7. EXT. GOLF COURSE – TEEING OFF – DAY (THREE)

Larry and Kenny G are teeing off. Jeff and GEOFF are standing beside the tee box. Larry walks up and drives the ball straight down the fairway. Kenny compliments Larry's shot and walks up to the tee.

Kenny: "Alright, step aside, let me show you how it's done."

Larry and Jeff stand back to watch Kenny's drive.

Geoff: "Okay Kenny, let's see that G-force."

Kenny hits his ball. Larry and Jeff shield their eyes from the sun to see where the ball went. Jeff says, "Perfect! Look at that, right next to mine!" Kenny puts his club back in his bag. Kenny and Geoff climb into the golf cart and make their way toward the fairway. Jeff and Larry start loading up their cart.

Larry (to Jeff): "So, you think he'll do it?"

Jeff: "Yeah he'll do it! He does stuff like that all the time."

8. EXT. GOLF COURSE – ON THE GREEN—LATER-DAY (THREE)

Larry, Jeff, and Geoff are standing on the edge of the green (having already finished the hole). Larry and Jeff begin to talk quietly. Kenny is walking around the edge of the green as if to look for his ball. Kenny pauses briefly over his ball, looks around (towards Jeff, Larry and Geoff) and kicks his ball onto the green from the fringe. Larry and Jeff both see this out of the corner of their eyes and shrug. Kenny quickly lines up his shot, sinks his ball and shouts, "Birdie!" He picks the ball up, throws it up, and catches it. His golf ball has a large letter 'G' printed on it. As Kenny catches his ball, he shows Jeff and Larry the 'G' on his ball.

Kenny: "Hey look, found the G-spot!"

Larry and Jeff both tease Kenny on his lame joke. Kenny puts his club back in his bag. Larry walks over to Kenny.

Larry: "I don't normally do this, but... I have a favor to ask."

Kenny (interested): "What is it?"

Larry: "It's my girlfriend's birthday next week and she'd love for you to...play for her. Just a song or two. She..."

Kenny (cuts Larry off): "I'd love to."

Larry (shocked): "Really? That was the quickest 'yes' I've ever got for a favor."

Kenny: "No Problem. It'll be fun!"

Kenny and Geoff get in their cart and drive away. Larry shouts over to Jeff, "He'll do it!" Jeff walks over to Larry.

Jeff: "What the fuck was that? The guy just kicks his ball closer to the hole?"

Larry: "Yeah, 'Birdie'...he should've called 'Bullshit'...I'm gonna ask him about it."

Jeff (hesitant): "He just agreed to do the concert for Rita. I know you'd want nothing more than to call him out, but don't fuck this up. Just coast from here on out. We only have a couple holes left."

Larry nods in agreement. They get in their cart and drive to the next hole.

9. EXT. GOLF COURSE –TEEING OFF - LATER-DAY (THREE)

Geoff is watching Jeff tee off. Kenny is looking for something in the pockets of his golf bag. Larry walks over to him.

Larry: "G('gee')...THE 'G' man...How's it going?"

Kenny comments on the perfect weather and says it's, "G('gee')-reat('rate')."

Larry looks at the sky and agrees. Larry leans closer to Kenny.

Larry: "You really like that 'G' thing, don't you? I couldn't help but notice you gave yourself a little...'help' at the last hole."

Kenny (confused): "Help? What are you talking about?"

Larry tells Kenny that he saw him tap the ball with his foot.

Kenny (shrugs/nods 'no'): "Doesn't ring a bell."

Larry: "So, when you're playing your...clarinet..."

Kenny (interrupts/corrects): "Sax, Larry. Soprano sax."

Larry: "Okay, sax. When you're playing and you make a mistake, do you just keep going? Or do you go back and correct the wrong note."

Kenny (confidently): "Oh, that's easy. I don't make mistakes."

Larry: "Okay so you DON'T make mistakes. But let's say, for the sake of conversation, you did. Would you...'kick' the notes back into place?"

Kenny: "I *DON'T* make mistakes."

Larry does the 'Lie-Eye-Stare' with Kenny and says, "Okay".

10. EXT. GOLF COURSE – PUTTING GREEN—LATER DAY (THREE)
Larry, Jeff, Geoff, and Kenny arrive at the spot where their golf balls landed near the green. They get out of their carts and head toward their golf balls in the fringe. Jeff claps.

Jeff: "Alright! Last hole!"

Jeff hits his ball onto the green. Kenny walks up to his ball and kneels down (studying the green).

Jeff: "Hey, first make it to the green."

Kenny laughs and lines himself up with his ball. He swings and it only goes a short distance (landing three feet from the green). Kenny walks up to his ball and looks around. He kicks his ball onto the green. Kenny stands back and tells Larry, "You're up." Larry arrives at and addresses his golf ball. Larry looks up from his ball and glares at Kenny, then back down at the ball. Larry stands up straight and kicks his ball onto the green with his foot. Kenny gives Larry a dirty look.

Larry: "What?"

Kenny: "Oh what? I accidentally bump the ball and now you start kicking yours?"

Larry starts arguing with Kenny about kicking the ball versus bumping the ball. Kenny walks up and kicks his own ball again.

Kenny: "There, see? Now we're even."

Larry kicks his own ball closer to the pin.

Kenny: "You just kicked your ball!"

Larry: "I didn't KICK it...I *BUMPED* IT."

Kenny kicks his own ball again. They both repeatedly kick their own balls while arguing. Eventually, Larry kicks his ball over to the hole and it goes in.

Larry (shouting/mocking): "BIRDIE!! IT'S A BIRDIE!! OHH, ONE UNDER PAR!!"

Kenny picks up his ball and climbs into his cart. He yells at Larry.

Kenny: "Good luck finding someone else to play for your girlfriend's birthday, asshole!"

Kenny speeds off in his golf cart. Geoff runs over to Larry.

Geoff: "What the fuck Larry?!"

Larry tries to tell Geoff how Kenny was cheating. Geoff doesn't believe it and complains that he doesn't have a ride back to the clubhouse now. Larry and Jeff tell Geoff that he can hop onto their cart. Geoff squeezes in next to Larry in their cart and they drive off.

11. INT. LARRY'S HOUSE – HALLWAY – DAY (FOUR)
Larry is standing outside the bathroom door. A **PLUMBER** is heard off-camera.

Plumber: "Got it! There's your problem. It's a...I think it's a...G-string."

Larry (confused): "What?"

The plumber walks out of the bathroom with a G-string hanging at the end of a plumber snake and says, "G-string." Larry looks over at Leon and points to the G-string.

Leon (shrugs): "What? That ain't mine."

Larry: "Well it sure isn't mine either. Given the number of women that you bring over here, I think I know how that got there."

Leon recalls who the G-string may belong to and walks away. Larry turns toward the plumber.

Larry: "Have you ever wondered what the 'G' in G-string stands for?"

Plumber: "To be honest, that's never crossed my mind."

Larry tries to think of what the 'G' could possibly stand for and names a string of words.

Larry: "Good? Glad? Gawking? Glory? Gum?..."

The plumber is unenthused and holds his hand out to signify that he wants his money.

Plumber: "That'll be $99.50."

Larry (laughing): "Huh, you pull panties out of a toilet and that's a hundred bucks right down the drain. Easiest job in the world."

Plumber: "Yeah (lengthy pause)...$99.50."

Larry: "And what's with the fifty cents? Why not make it an even hundred? Ever notice that? Water, $2.99! Toilet Paper, $9.95! Really? How hard is it to round up?"

The plumber holds out his hand again. Larry hands him a hundred-dollar bill. The plumber asks if he wants the change.

Larry: "Round it up. See how I did that? Round UP???"

The plumber takes the G-string off the plumber snake and puts it in his pocket. Larry stares and shakes his head (giving the plumber a disgusted look).

12. INT. LARRY'S HOUSE – LIVING ROOM – DAY (FOUR)

Larry is on the phone apologizing to Kenny G. Larry asks if there's anything he can do to make up for it and to get Kenny to play for Rita.

Kenny: "Well, there is one thing..."

Kenny tells Larry that he has an eye doctor appointment the next day and he's getting his eyes dilated. Kenny explains that won't be able to drive because of the procedure. He asks Larry to do him a favor and drive him to his appointment and back. Larry agrees. Kenny tells Larry he will pick him up in his car the next day.

Kenny: "I have a silver Infiniti...the 'G' Series."

Larry (mocking): "G('gee')...what a surprise."

Kenny: "I'll see you tomorrow."

13. EXT. KENNY G'S CAR – DRIVING – DAY (FIVE)
Larry and Kenny are walking towards Kenny's car.

Kenny: "You wanna drive THE 'G'?" (Without waiting for a response from Larry, he immediately tosses the key to him).

< SCENE TRANSITION >

Larry is driving Kenny G to his eye doctor appointment. Kenny is listening to his own music on the stereo.

Kenny: "Hold on, this is my favorite part."

Kenny turns up the volume and listens to his own sax solo. After the solo is over, he turns the music down and says, "Genius."

Larry (laughing sarcastically): "Yeah, it's something alright."

Kenny reaches in the backseat and pulls out a saxophone. He tells Larry he always carries one with him because "you never know when inspiration might strike." Kenny begins to play his sax as Larry drives. Larry is staring straight ahead gritting his teeth in annoyance. As Kenny is playing, he starts to get into it and turns the sax toward Larry. Larry grips the wheel tighter and is noticeably annoyed.

Larry's phone rings and Kenny stops playing as Larry answers it. Larry puts his phone on speaker -- it's Leon calling.

Leon: "LD, where's the panties? The G-string that clogged the toilet, where is it?"

Kenny: "GEE-string??"

Larry (annoyed/ignoring Kenny): "I don't know...the plumber took them. Why?"

Leon (yelling): "This bitch called me up and I told her I found her panties, and she's all yellin' and shit. She's on her way over right now to pick them up."

Larry: "Well, what do you want me to do?! I'm in the car with Kenny G right now...I'm taking him to the eye doctor."

Leon (excited): "Kenny motha-fuckin' G? Hey G...you out there tappin' ass? Mmmm! I was tellin' Larry, you destroy the pussy left and right!"

Kenny plays a few notes on his sax.

Kenny: "Well, I don't know about 'destroying'."

Leon: "Kenny fuckin' G. Alright, this bitch is here and about to tear up my ass."

A woman heard indistinctly yelling in the background of Leon's phone call. Leon begins to yell back and hangs up the phone. Larry arrives at the doctor's office and pulls into a parking space.

14. EXT. KENNY G'S CAR – DRIVING—LATER DAY (FIVE)

Larry is driving Kenny back from the eye doctor. Kenny has special protective glasses on because his eyes were dilated. Larry comments on how Kenny looks like the "Jewish terminator" with the glasses on. Kenny laughs at Larry's comment. As Larry is driving, he receives a text message from Rita. The text reads, "DONT FORGET MY BIG ART SHOW IS TODAY! SEE YOU THERE!"

Larry: "Shit! Rita's art gallery! I completely forgot! My girlfriend's got this art show, I promised her I'd be there! I totally forgot!"

Kenny: "What? Where is this art show?"

Larry (excited): "I've got you in the car...and you've got your flute..."

Kenny (interrupting/irritated): "Sax, Larry. Soprano Sax."

Larry: "Whatever. This is great! Would you mind if we made a quick stop? We'll pop in and pop out. You can play a few notes and she'll go crazy."

Kenny: "I wouldn't mind at all, I love art! Let's do it! Let's 'G.'-'O.' ('gee-ohh')!"

Larry glares at Kenny for making another 'G' pun. Kenny makes a comment on how he'll look weird with the protective eye glasses on. Larry accelerates and passes numerous cars (driving aggressively).

15. INT. ART GALLERY – MAIN FLOOR – DAY (FIVE)

Larry and Kenny enter through the doors of Rita's art gallery. There are a number of vagina paintings hanging on the walls, as well as vagina sculptures of all shapes and sizes on display pedestals throughout the gallery. Kenny looks at the sculptures, looks at Larry and back at the sculptures. He (momentarily) raises his glasses away from his eyes.

Kenny: "Wow! Are those..."

Larry (interrupting): "Wait over there for my cue."

Kenny (holding his sax) walks over to the spot and looks at a sculpture. Rita walks up to Larry.

Rita: "Larry. Glad you could make it! Look at this turn out. There are SO MANY people here."

Larry: "Yeah...I hope you don't mind, I brought a friend."

Larry points over to Kenny and Kenny begins to play a song on his sax.

Rita (shrieking): "LARRY!"

The room gets silent and everyone turns toward Kenny. Kenny is slowly walking toward Rita, swaying to his music. The crowd claps as Kenny gets into his song. As Kenny approaches Rita, he pauses near a six-foot-tall vagina sculpture. Kenny (swaying to his music) swings his sax around and it bumps into a vagina sculpture. The vagina sculpture tips over (in slow motion), falls to the ground and shatters into a thousand pieces. The gallery crowd reacts in shock and horror. Kenny's sax squeaks (hits an 'off' note) and he stops playing. The crowd is silent. Kenny looks at the shattered remains, then looks at Larry. Larry has a look of pain on his face. Larry looks at Rita. She's standing still, her mouth hanging open in shock.

An **OLD MAN** in the gallery (asks): "What's going on?"

A **YOUNG WOMAN** in the gallery (replies): "He destroyed it!"

An **OLD WOMAN** in the gallery (asks): "Who?"

The **OLD MAN** in the gallery (asks): "Destroyed what?"

Larry (half-smiling and nodding his head): "Kenny G *destroyed* THE pussy."

FADE OUT/Cue Music.

(END)

- 20 -

We're Not in Kansas Anymore

The following episode, "(Almost) No Place Like Home", started out in our usual manner. We found inspiration (for a 'regular'/26 minute episode) in characters we encountered on Hollywood Boulevard. That area (the theaters, the clubs, the Walk of Fame) was an immense source of material and ideas for us (John and Ray). As we wrote out scenes and continued gathering ideas, 'No Place' grew to such length that we revised it as a two-part episode. And then it grew even larger. After reviewing the impressive length of the first draft of 'No Place' episode, we discussed separating it from the book and presenting it to the Curb Your Enthusiasm production company as a full-length feature film (Curb Your Enthusiasm – THE MOVIE!)

The initial 'No Place' episode made clever use of a few cameo / guest-star appearances. Rather quickly, the list grew to more than a dozen guest stars and we realized the potential of the storyline made for an incredible (extra-long) finale episode (should Curb ever come to an end).

We took an iconic, landmark (musical) film from the past and used/substituted Curb Your Enthusiasm cast members to parody the film's original characters. We crafted a fast-paced string of 3-act plays tied together using much of the original films plot, creating an exceptionally inspired final episode. '(Almost) No Place Like Home' weaves in highlights from all 9 seasons of Curb Your Enthusiasm to reward fans and loyal viewers with a satisfying and memorable GRAND FINALE (to '*THE WORLDS GREATEST*' comedy series, EVER!).

It was during the creation of '(Almost) No Place Like Home' that Los Angeles, which started out as our second home, had become a permanent fixture. We regularly meet with producers, directors, writers, agents and attend many Hollywood functions. It's the ideal place to promote our creativity and where we made our (unexpected) screen debut on Curb Your Enthusiasm. Was it hard, tiresome and time consuming work? Absolutely. Would we'd do it all over again? In a heartbeat! We've met some of Hollywood's top talent and were invited to many events, private parties, concerts etc. that gave us visibility, and more importantly, put us on the path to unlocking the age old Hollywood cliché: *It's not WHAT you know…it's WHO you know.*

While living in Chicago, the harsh winters kept us locked inside and motivated us to create some of the funniest material we've ever written. Over and over, Ray kept saying to John, 'Envision IT' until the day we received THE call. We flew to LA and met with an Executive Producer of Curb Your Enthusiasm. An extended discussion took place and resulted in our returning to Los Angeles a few weeks later to participate in Season 9. A BONUS — we made a cameo appearance in the final Curb episode (#10) of the season. Call it a dream or what you will…we call it hard work. We now call LA home…**and there truly is**…

21

Episode 10 – *The FINALE*

"(Almost) No Place Like Home"

Synopsis: Brought on by an unpredictable accident, Larry has an out-of-body experience with the surreal-ness of a psychedelic episode.

Scenes: 13

Cast: Larry(Dorothy), Leon(The Wiz), Cheryl(Glinda, the Good Witch), Jeff(Lion), Susie(the Wicked Witch), Marty Funkhouser(Tin Man), Richard Lewis(Scarecrow), Wanda Sykes(Guardian of the Gate), Sammi Green, Guest(Latisha).

Special Guests: Peter Dinklage as the Dwarf, Tyrion Lannister; Mel Brooks (The Real Wiz); Ted Danson, Mary Steenburgen, Richard Kind (Winged Monkey), the Rat Dog.

Robert Weide (Bathroom Attendant inside the Wiz's castle). Jeff Schaffer (Tour-map Salesman on the Path of Stars).

Talking Trees: Jerry Seinfeld, Jason Alexander, Julia Louis-Dreyfus, Michael Richards.

Hall of Doors (The Doors of a *Different* Color) **Guests**:

> Ellia English (Auntie Rae)
> Bill Buckner as himself
> Paul Sand (Chef Guy Bernier)
> Dana Lee (Mr. Takahashi)
> Catherine O'Hara (Bam Bam Funkhouser)
> Rosie O'Donnell as herself
> Anne Bedian (Shara)
> Gina Gershon (Anna, the Dry Cleaner)
> Robert Weide (Larry David)

"Almost No Place Like Home"

1. INT. LARRY'S BEDROOM – NIGHT (ONE)

[Scene is 'detuned' of color/hues --- giving the appearance of all earth-tones, without being complete black & white.]

LARRY walks through the front door of his house pulling a rolling suitcase. He closes the door behind him. **LEON (JB SMOOVE)** greets him.

Leon (shouts): "HEY! LD...Welcome Back!"

Larry (sniffing): "What's that smell?...It smells like...strawberries...and cotton candy."

Leon: "It's Latisha taking a bubble bath...some aromatherapy shit...mmm, delicious!"

Larry: "You don't have a tub in your bathroom."

Leon: "Nope. She's usin' yours."

Larry: "Jesus! I don't want ANYONE using my bathroom."

Larry shouts back to Leon that he is too tired to care and goes up the stairs.

< SCENE TRANSITION >

Larry passes **LATISHA (Un-named GUEST STAR)** (wearing Larry's monogrammed robe) in the hallway. She looks Larry up and down.

Latisha: "You must be LD."

Larry: "You must be Strawberry Shortcake."

Latisha checks out Larry's ass as he passes. Larry enters his bedroom and sighs (deep breath).

Larry (standing in his bedroom) picks up a golf putter drags several golf balls to the middle of the room. He lines up a shot towards a golf putting machine across the room. Larry hits the ball into the device and it forcefully sends the ball back to him. Larry lines up for another putt. As Larry swings the club to putt, Leon is heard (off-screen, interrupting Larry's swing).

Leon (heard off-screen): "LD! Storm comin'. Windows on the Prius are down. You should roll them up before it rains."

Larry's putt misses the return machine by a wide margin. Larry bangs the club down in frustration (a loud 'thump' is heard).

Leon (heard off-screen): "What was that noise?"

Larry: "Never mind. YOU DO IT...take care of the windows. You treat this place like it's (your) home, so take responsibility for something."

Larry lines up another golf ball and swings the club to putt. Leon is heard (off-screen, interrupting Larry's swing).

Leon (heard off-screen): "You mean, like, right now?"

Larry's putt (again) misses the return machine by a wide margin. Larry bangs the club down in frustration (a loud 'thump' is heard).

Leon (heard off-screen): "There's that thump again. LD, you thumpin' Latisha?"

Larry ignores Leon. Larry lines up another golf ball, swings the club back to putt and pauses, expecting Leon will interrupt. Larry swings and hits the golf ball into the return machine and the ball does not return/remains stuck in machine. Larry bends over to look into the machine. [Change camera angle from wide shot to Larry's point-of-view looking into the machine at the stuck ball.]

Larry can see the ball stuck in the machine. [Change camera angle back to wide shot.]

Larry straightens up and takes a step towards the machine. He (accidentally) steps on a golf ball, loses his footing and falls backward onto the carpeting, looking up at the ceiling. Larry groans. His head turns to the side, looking directly at the putting machine.
[Change camera angle from wide shot to Larry's point-of-view looking directly into the machine at the stuck ball.]

A loud click is heard (audio dub) and the ball forcefully ejects towards Larry's head. A loud thump is heard (audio dub). Larry groans [fade to black].

Leon (audio only): "LD...LD???"

(Audio dub:) A loud thunder clap is heard.

Cue intro music (Frolic), logos and opening credits.
Opening credit ends with a parody of MGM-logo film opening, replacing the lion with a black swan roaring.

2. INT-EXT. LARRY'S HOUSE – LIVINGROOM – DAY (DREAM SEQUENCE)

[Scene is 'detuned' of color/hues --- giving the appearance of all earth-tones, without being complete black & white.]

[Fade in - blur through black]

Larry is walking down the stairs. A tapping noise is heard followed by (faint) giggling of (various) high pitched voices. The noise abruptly stops. Larry looks at the front door and calls out.

Larry: "Leon? Is that you?? If you're out there screwing around with your girlfriend, I'm throwing the two of you…" (interrupted/trails off).

The noise (tapping and giggling) is briefly heard again and Larry walks to his front door. [Camera angle changes to over-the-shoulder.] Larry opens the door [color change - earth-tone colors are replaced with vibrant colors] and is confronted by a vividly colored scene of flowers and trees. Larry (looking around in amazement) steps outside and takes in the beauty of the vibrant world in front of him. A voice is heard: "GREETINGS." Larry is mesmerized by his surroundings and does not appear to hear the greeting. Larry takes another step forward. A voice is heard(yelling): "Hey! What the fuck!" Larry is startled and quickly steps back. Larry looks left, then right, and then (slowly) downward and sees a **DWARF.**

[The **DWARF** is **Peter Dinklage**, dressed as Tyrion Lannister from Game of Thrones].

Dwarf/Tyrion: "Watch where you're stepping with those ...things." (pointing to Larry's feet. [Camera close-up] Larry is wearing hideous red shoes). Larry (looks down) stares at his red shoes for a few seconds.

Larry: "Pretty, Pretty, Pretty Red."

Dwarf/Tyrion: "Pretty, pretty UGLY...if you ask me."

Larry (confused): "What are you doing on my...front step? Where IS my front step? What is this place?"

Dwarf/Tyrion (in an 'American' accent): "That, I can't tell you, but find the Wiz and he will..."

Larry (interrupting): "The Wiz? Really? THE Wiz?"

Dwarf/Tyrion (in a 'British/Irish' accent): "AYE. THE Wiz. Find the Wiz and he, sir, will grant your request."

Larry (laughing): "Request? What request?"

Dwarf/Tyrion (in an 'American' accent): "Well, you wanna go home don't you?"

Larry (confused): "I don't think going home (Larry gestures behind himself) is that big of a concern."

Larry turns to show Tyrion his house, but it has disappeared. Larry rapidly turns around in a full circle, his mouth open in astonishment. Larry turns back to the direction where Tyrion was standing, but Tyrion has also disappeared. In his place is a (double flap) wicker basket covered with a blue and white checkered handkerchief. A paper-scroll is attached to the handle. Larry takes the scroll off the basket, unrolls it and (appears to) read it.

(Audio dub of Tyrion's voice, with a 'British' accent):

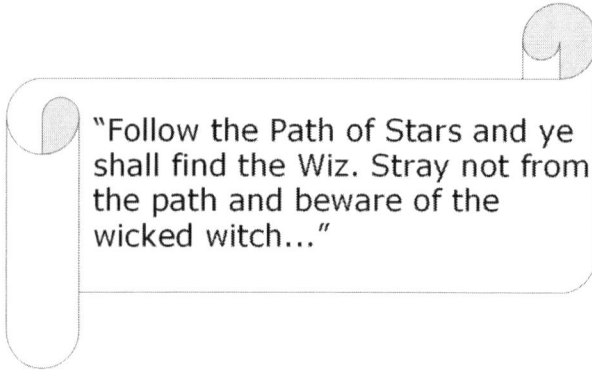

"Follow the Path of Stars and ye shall find the Wiz. Stray not from the path and beware of the wicked witch..."

Larry: "Stray not??? Who does this guy think he is...Ricky Gervais?"

Larry finds an inscription on the inside flap of the basket. (Audio dub of Tyrion's voice, with an 'American' accent): "You're probably wondering, 'what's with the basket?'; In your time of need, reach in and you will pull out your salvation."

Larry laughs and shakes his head. He rolls up the scroll and looks inside. The basket appears to be empty. Larry turns the basket upside down and shakes it. Larry tosses the scroll inside. As he closes the flap, he sees an object inside. Larry opens the flap on the basket and reaches inside. He pulls out a box of Girl Scout cookies. He (again) looks inside the basket and the scroll is gone. He puts the box back and closes the basket. Larry lifts his foot to take a step towards The Path (a sign is stuck in the ground announcing: 'This way to The Path of Stars').

< SCENE TRANSITION >

As he puts his foot down, the scene immediately transitions to 6700 Hollywood Blvd/the Hollywood Walk of Fame*.

[* – The star located 6700 Hollywood Blvd is dedicated to Frank Morgan. Frank Morgan played the role of The Wizard in the movie, *The Wizard of Oz*.]

(Audio dub of Tyrion's voice, with a 'British' accent): "Follow the Path of Stars and ye shall find the Wiz."

Larry is immediately approached by a **Hollywood Tour-Map Seller (JEFF SCHAFFER)**.

Tour-Map Seller: "Hey! First time in Hollywood? How about a map to the Stars homes?...all the Seinfeld cast homes are on it. Only ten bucks."

Larry steps back, waving the seller away.

Tour-Map Seller: "Five bucks?...Three?...Gimmee a buck? C'mon. How about a quarter?"

Larry: "Nahh...not a fan of that show...never cared for the cast."

Larry sidesteps the map-seller.

Larry: "I have a feeling I'm not in Brentwood anymore. I must be somewhere...somewhere over the rainbow?"

Larry begins walking along The Path of Stars.

3. EXT. PATH OF STARS – INTRO TO THE GOOD WITCH – DAY (DREAM SEQUENCE)

Larry is walking along The Path/Hollywood Walk of Fame. Larry pauses when he sees a large bubble floating towards him. As the bubble gets close, it 'pops' (audio dub: 'finger-mouth' popping noise). **CHERYLWITCH (CHERYL HINES)** appears. CherylWitch, dressed in a sparkling, sexy, low-cut dress, is holding a wand, and wearing a tiara. Larry smiles, fixated by her beauty.

Cheryl: "Let me ask you somethin'...What's with the cutesy basket?"

Larry: (oblivious to her question): "Let me ask YOU somethin'...What's with the bubble?"

CherylWitch introduces herself.

CherylWitch: "I'm the good witch of the North...Glinda-Anastasia-Cordelia-Cherylesque-Daveedess."

Larry: "Umm, Glindastastia-what?...S'pose I call you Cheryl."

Larry takes her hand, kisses it and introduces himself.

Larry (while looking her 'up and down'): "I'm Larry. Pleased to meet you...'Good' witch, you say? Pretty, Pretty Good."

CherylWitch (frustrated tone): "Yeah Larry, the GOOD witch. Let me ask you somethin'...What's *IN* the cutesy basket?"

Larry reaches into the basket and pulls out a bouquet of flowers. A card is attached to the bottom (camera close up) with the words 'Ida Funkhouser' printed on it. Larry yanks the card off and gives the bouquet to CherylWitch. CherylWitch accepts the flowers while glaring at the card in Larry's hand.

CherylWitch: "Thanks for the *empty* gesture, Larry."

Larry ignores the comment and asks if she knows the Wiz and where he can find him?

CherylWitch: "Yes...the great and wonderful Wiz himself. He lives up there (points towards the Hollywood sign), in Emerald Canyon...let's see, you take the 405 to the 101, past the 134 cutoff, and then...well, it's a long journey. Just follow the Path of Stars and you will find him."

CherylWitch: "Good luck on your journey to see the Wiz."

Larry: "Yeah...I hope I can pop your bubble again sometime."

CherylWitch (image inside a 'bubble and voice trailing off): "The sooner you get out of Hollywood altogether, the safer you'll sleep."

They both look at each other (extended gaze) and smile. CherylWitch vanishes. Larry continues walking along The Path of Stars.

4. EXT. PATH OF STARS – INTRO TO RICHARDCROW – DAY (DREAM SEQUENCE)

Larry is walking down the Path of Stars and appears to trip

over something. Larry looks down and sees [camera close-up] someone's foot extending into the path. The camera pans back from the foot and reveals it's **RICHARDCROW** (**Richard Lewis**). RichardCrow is dressed similar to a scarecrow (in dirty/ratty clothes and hat). RichardCrow is sitting on the ground/against a storefront, holding a liquor bottle in a paper bag. Larry nudges RichardCrow's shoulder and RichardCrow looks up at Larry. RichardCrow appears intoxicated/slurring his words (angry for being disturbed). RichardCrow holds the (empty) bottle up to take a sip, discovers it's empty and shakes it over his mouth as if to get every last drop. RichardCrow desperately pleads for a drink and asks Larry if he has any booze.

RichardCrow: "Mister. You got any hooch in that faggoty man-basket?"

Larry: "Hooch?"

Larry reaches in to the basket and pulls out an open 'takeout' container filled with shrimp.

Larry (offering the box): "Shrimp?"

RichardCrow: "Shrimp? What are you, DEAF? HOOCH! I need a drink."

Larry comments on the smell coming from RichardCrow and suggests he inhale the fumes off his clothes.

Larry: "Who are you?...and WHAT are you?"

RichardCrow (slurring his words): "I'm...I'm...I'm FUCKING thirsty."

RichardCrow holds up his empty bottle of booze and shakes it to show Larry that it's empty.

Larry introduces himself.

Larry (grinning): "Hello, Fucking Thirsty...I'm Larry." (Larry extends out his hand.)

RichardCrow (groaning/reaching up): "Jesus Christ" RichardCrow extends out his filthy hand.

Larry: "YOU'RE JESUS?"

Larry observes RichardCrow's filthy hand, retracts his own hand and places it in his pocket.

RichardCrow: "No. I'm...crow...crowRichard...crow... RichardCrow. And I'm a failure 'cause I haven't got a drink." (shakes empty bottle of booze turned upside down; RichardCrow struggles to his feet.)

(Fade in AUDIO: 'If I Only Had A Brain' music from The Wizard of Oz). RichardCrow begins to sing and dance/shuffle.

RichardCrow (singing/dancing): *"I would only be so happy, a drunk who's only slappy, if I only had a drink (gestures with bag-bottle)...I could take a little sip...or have a tiny nip, if I only..."*

Larry displays a pained look on his face, waves his hands in front of him and cuts off RichardCrow.

Larry: "Alright, I get it. You want a drink. I GET IT."

RichardCrow: "So...What's your deal?"

Larry: "I'm on my way to see this Wiz guy."

RichardCrow claims he's heard of the Wiz.

RichardCrow (out of breath): "So...this Wiz guy, do you think he has anything to drink at his place...some booze...or cough medicine...maybe some Nyquil, or something?"

Larry (laughing): "I'm afraid you've already had too much."

RichardCrow: "Afraid? You're afraid? I'm not afraid. I'm not afraid of anything...except maybe an open flame. Ahhh...what the fuck do you know? You and your creepy red shoes–you look like a geriatric Ronald McDonald child predator...especially with your...(belch)...little girly basket. I wanna see this Wiz guy. I need a drink...let's go."

Larry and RichardCrow begin walking up the street. RichardCrow moves closer to Larry as they walk. Larry glances (sideways) at RichardCrow and moves away (as they walk). RichardCrow (again) moves closer to Larry and Larry glances (sideways) at RichardCrow and (again) moves away.

5. EXT. PATH OF STARS – INTRO TO TINFUNK - DAY (DREAM SEQUENCE)

RichardCrow stops, leans on a storefront and announces he needs a break. Larry turns to look at him. In the entryway of the storefront (a welding shop) is a metal statue-like figure. Larry approaches the statue (**BOB EINSTEIN as TINFUNK,** wearing a metal/Tinman 'suit'). The statue-man

(Funkhouser/TinFunk) is attached to a metal post. Larry examines the statue. He taps on it with a (closed) hand. Each time he taps, an 'echo' of the same number of taps is heard (in return). Larry taps 5 times [in the shave-and-a-hair-cut rhythm]. Two taps are heard in response. Larry looks closer at the metal suit-man and attempts to rotate the head.

TinFunk: "Don't do that."

Larry (startled): "Who said that?"

TinFunk: "I did. Don't do that. I'm not some cheap doll. My head doesn't come off. I need some help here."

TinFunk asks for Larry to help him by breaking him away from the post and setting him free. Larry complies and breaks TinFunk loose/away from the post. TinFunk squeaks when he moves and asks Larry for some oil. Larry says he has no oil.

TinFunk (squeaking/grinding): "What's in the sissy basket?"

Larry pauses, reaches into the basket (searching) and pulls out a soiled, limp fifty-dollar bill.

Larry (offering it to TinFunk): "No oil, but maybe you can buy some with this?

TinFunk (backing away/squeaking): "That's FILTHY. Don't you have a fresh one? I'm not taking that fifty. No. Not that one."

Larry offers it to RichardCrow.

Larry (to RichardCrow): "Hooch money?"

RichardCrow refuses it.

RichardCrow: "Not even a bum would take that."

Larry puts the fifty-dollar bill back into the basket and pulls out a pair of LA Dodger game tickets.

Larry: "It's all I have. You're welcome to them."

TinFunk thanks Larry for the offer but says he doesn't have much to live for. Larry asks TinFunk why he's so down. TinFunk (unenthusiastically/slow/lethargic voice), says he doesn't know---he feels depressed, as if he's empty inside.

[*In background*: RichardCrow picks up a can [camera close-up] marked 'Ethyl-Oil – 12 % Alcohol by Volume". He looks at TinFunk, pauses, sniffs it, and then gulps it.]

TinFunk: "Go ahead -- tap on my chest. It's hollow."

Larry: "Maybe you just need a wife or girlfriend?"

TinFunk: "I'm afraid I'm a little rusty."

Larry: "I know what's missing...you need some SPUNK!"

Larry asks TinFunk for his name.

TinFunk: "They all just call me TinFunk...I don't like it."

Larry: "I think I'll call you...SPUNKMAN!"

Larry tells TinFunk/Spunkman he needs to find some guy called the Wiz, in order to get home.

TinFunk: "Why don't you just call a cab?"

Larry: "Let me ask you something...do you know this Wiz guy?"

Larry explains that the Wiz is the only one that can grant him his wish to go home. TinFunk says the name sounds familiar but he's not sure.

TinFunk: "Listen, I have a favor to ask..."

Larry (scoffs/interrupts): "What are you nuts? I just DID you a favor, a BIG favor....and now you're asking for another? You know what you are? YOU...are a favor ABUSER."

TinFunk: "That was not a favor. You freed me. That was a gesture. Those are two completely different things."

Larry argues with TinFunk about the difference between a gesture and a favor.

Larry: "Jesus. You can't make a gesture to a TinFunk without them taking advantage of it."

TinFunk: "Enough! Look, are you willing to help me or not?"

Larry (shrugs): "Eh."

RichardCrow: "Yeah! Larry's right. Who...who are you anyway? How do we know you're (belch) not just some... clinking, clanking, clattering collection of caliginous junk?" RichardCrow knocks on TinFunk's metal body.

TinFunk (angry): "Don't do that."

Larry (to RichardCrow): "Caliginous?"

TinFunk announces he's going with them because he wants to ask the Wiz for some SPUNK. Larry doesn't want TinFunk along and argues with him. TinFunk insists he must go with them on the journey to see the Wiz.

(Fade in AUDIO: 'If I Only Had A Brain' music from The Wizard of Oz.) TinFunk begins to sing/shuffle(squeaking).

TinFunk (singing/dancing): *"I wouldn't be a punk, and I'd shake this state of funk, if I only had some SPUNK (pounds his chest with his fist)...You wouldn't think me feeble, or a sleepy little beagle if I only..."*

Larry has a pained look on his face, waves his hands in front of him and cuts off TinFunk.

Larry: "Alright, I get it. You want spunk, I GET IT."

Larry relents. Larry, RichardCrow and TinFunk walk up the street/The Path (away from the camera). TinFunk looks down at Larry's feet as they walk and makes a comment about Larry's red shoes.

TinFunk: "Would you JUST look at those shoes...you really think someone will grant you a wish wearing those...It's like you're wearing insults on your feet."

Larry, RichardCrow and TinFunk continue walking up the street. TinFunk moves closer to Larry as they walk. Larry glances (sideways) at TinFunk and moves away (as they walk). TinFunk (again) moves closer to Larry and Larry glances (sideways) at TinFunk and (again) moves away.

6. EXT. PATH OF STARS – INTRO TO JEFFLION & SUSIEWITCH – DAY/DARKER (DREAM SEQUENCE)

The sun is setting on The Path of Stars [Hollywood or Sunset Boulevard]. Larry, RichardCrow, and TinFunk are walking up the street. A loud 'crunching' noise is heard and they stop walking.

TinFunk: "Do you hear that?"

RichardCrow: "Hear what? How could anyone hear ANYTHING with your squeaky fucking shoes. Get some oil in your diet for Chrisssakes."

TinFunk points in the direction of the noise.

RichardCrow: "Look! There. It's SASQUATCH."

They walk closer and encounter **JEFFLION (JEFF GARLIN** -- his back toward them/facing away, he is dressed poorly, as a shabby, worn down lion). JeffLion has his face buried in a large bag of potato chips and is 'forcefully' eating them.

JeffLion is startled by the three of them approaching. JeffLion turns around (shaking/nervous/looking in all directions) and wipes the chips stuck to his face with his hand/paw (bits remain).

JeffLion (cradling the bag of chips, SHOUTS): "HEEYYYYY! My chips. MINE."

Larry: "Who are you?"

JeffLion (shaking/stuttering): "J...J---Jef...JeffLion."

RichardCrow and TinFunk want to know why JeffLion is so nervous and scared.

Larry: "I'd be a little concerned too if I looked like that."

JeffLion (backing up): "The wicked witch is coming...the wicked witch is coming!"

Larry, RichardCrow and TinFunk all assure JeffLion there is no such thing as wicked witches.

[Audio dub: sound of thunder. A puff of smoke appears in front of them. Audio dub music track: 'For whom the bell tolls' by Gianni Ferrio.]

SUSIEWITCH (SUSIE ESSMAN) appears as the wicked witch (wearing full green makeup) and curses at Larry, TinFunk, RichardCrow and specifically at JeffLion.

SusieWitch approaches them.

SusieWitch: "Look at all of you...pathetic...what the fuck is this? And look at you (pointing to RichardCrow) you're a fucking drunk. *I'll stuff an OLIVE with you.* And you (pointing to TinFunk), you rusted out bucket of shit, *I'll make a WHEELCHAIR out of you.*"

SusieWitch looks over at Larry and looks down to see his basket and red shoes.

SusieWitch (shaking her head): "And you...a grown man with a little wicker basket...and those ruby red...those look like MY shoes you cross-dressing sick fuck...Give me those ruby slippers...I'm the only one who knows how to use them you four-eyed, bald-headed, good-for-nothing asshole!" SusieWitch gets a 'shock' (audio dub: crackling noise) reaching for the red slippers.

Larry steps back from SusieWitch and reaches into the basket. He pulls his hand out of the basket and he's holding a cup of Pinkberry frozen yogurt. Larry (perplexed) stares at the cup.

Larry (gestures with the cup to SusieWitch): "Pinkberry? (pause) No good??"

JeffLion grabs the cup from Larry's hand.

JeffLion: "I'll take that."

SusieWitch looks over at JeffLion. JeffLion (shaking) smiles, nods and timidly waves at Susie.

JeffLion: "H...H...Hey."

SusieWitch: (turns to face JeffLion): "Shut your fat fucking face, you're next. That Pinkberry wasn't meant for you, you spineless flabby moron."

SusieWitch takes a step towards JeffLion. JeffLion (noticeably shaking) runs and hides behind a (thin/narrow) nearby tree.

SusieWitch (yelling): "Get back here you fat piece of shit! You're not a lion, you're a big pussy!"

RichardCrow leans forward and throws up in front of SusieWitch. SusieWitch jumps back. SusieWitch (angry) looks down and slowly looks up at RichardCrow.

TinFunk (to RichardCrow): "Your vomit is corroding my tin. Handiwipe??"

SusieWitch: "I'll get you...I'll get ALL of you...You make me sick! And (pointing at JeffLion hiding behind a tree) don't think I forgot about you, you fat fuck! If you had ANY balls, I'd take them and thumbtack them to my wall. You'll regret the day you ever met me."

SusieWitch disappears in a cloud of smoke. Larry, RichardCrow, and TinFunk are looking at each other in confusion. JeffLion rejoins them.

JeffLion: "She's an *angel*..."

RichardCrow: "An angel...*FROM HELL*."

Larry: "What a bitch."

SusieWitch (audio only): "I heard that, you bald prick."

JeffLion states he desperately wants courage. TinFunk suggests that JeffLion go with them on the journey to see the Wiz and the Wiz will give JeffLion some balls. Larry doesn't want JeffLion going along and argues with TinFunk, and JeffLion.

JeffLion: "I want to go. I need to go. I gotta get some...Balls!"

(Fade in AUDIO: 'If I Only Had The Nerve' music from The Wizard of Oz.) JeffLion begins to sing/dance (shuffle).

JeffLion (singing/dancing): "*I wouldn't be a pussy, and I wouldn't be so wussy, if I only had some BALLS...(grabs his crotch area). You wouldn't think me prissy or a girlie little sissy if I ...*"

Larry has a pained look on his face, waves his hands in front of him and cuts off JeffLion.

Larry: "Alright, I get it. You want BALLS. I GET IT."

Larry: "Let's get moving, it's getting dark."

TinFunk: "We're off to see the Wiz."

RichardCrow: "Speaking of wiz...I gotta drain *Little Richard*."

Larry (to RichardCrow): "Not now!"

Larry, RichardCrow, TinFunk, and JeffLion begin walking up the street. JeffLion moves closer to Larry as they walk. Larry glances (sideways) at JeffLion and moves away (as they walk). JeffLion (again) moves closer to Larry and Larry glances (sideways) at JeffLion and (again) moves away.

7. EXT. HOLLYWOOD FOREVER CEMETERY-'FOREST' SCENE – NIGHT (DREAM SEQUENCE)
Larry, RichardCrow, JeffLion, TinFunk enter a wooded area (Hollywood Forever Cemetery) and pause in front of a crypt-site (Judy Garland).

TinFunk: "I don't like this forest...it's dark and creepy."

Larry (pointing to the Judy Garland headstone and squinting): "Does that say 'Jeff Garlin'?"

RichardCrow breaks away from the group and stumbles over to a tree.

RichardCrow: "Nature's CALLING...gotta answer."

RichardCrow stands in front of a tree and unzips his pants. He is startled by a disgruntled yell ('HEY'). RichardCrow looks around and the voice/yell is heard again ('HEY').

RichardCrow looks up at the tree he is standing in front of. **JERRYTREE (JERRY SEINFELD)** opens his eyes and looks down at RichardCrow.

JerryTree: "What do you think you're doing? Zip up those pants."

RichardCrow stumbles backwards into another tree. He is startled by another voice.

ELAINETREE (Julia Louis-Dreyfus) yells: "Hey, watch it, mister!"

RichardCrow stumbles away from the tree and sits down on a tree stump.

GEORGESTUMP (Jason Alexander) sternly shouts: "Do you mind?!! RESPECT the wood."

RichardCrow: "Maybe I should quit drinking."

JerryTree throws apples at RichardCrow. RichardCrow tosses his empty booze bottle at JerryTree. **KRAMERTREE (Michael Richards)** falls into the shot and leans up against JerryTree.

KramerTree (smiling): "Hey, how's it goin'? Listen, uhhhh, Jerry, can I borrow an apple?"

Without waiting for a response, KramerTree rips an apple off JerryTree and takes a bite. ElaineTree throws an apple at GeorgeStump.

ElaineTree (laughing), "Hey stumpy! How about them apples?"

GeorgeStump: (Mocking laugh) "Ha, Ha, Ha. Very funny Elaine. You Know I can't reproduce apples."

The four trees throw apples at each other while arguing. Larry (perplexed) is looking at the chaos. The four trees stop arguing and begin throwing apples at Larry, RichardCrow, TinFunk, and JeffLion.

RichardCrow (to Larry): "Larry, hey, a little help here? Don't just stand there like a putz! Do something!"

Larry reaches into his basket (feels around) and pulls out a 5-wood golf club. He drives several apples back towards the trees.

Larry: "I respect wood...*THE* 5-WOOD."

TinFunk: "Where did you get that 5-Wood? That's my father's club, isn't it?"

RichardCrow: "Come on already. (belches) Let's get the fuck out of here."

Larry, RichardCrow, and TinFunk and JeffLion leave the talking tree forest.

8. INT. DUNGEON ROOM WITH SUSIEWITCH AND (INTRO OF) WINGED MONKEY – NIGHT (DREAM SEQUENCE)

SusieWitch is looking into her crystal ball-TV (a mirror-like flat screen TV). SusieWitch is talking to her crystal TV (swearing) and commands 'the screen' to show her 'that fat fuck Lion and his pathetic friends'. The crystal-TV screen image shows Larry, RichardCrow, TinFunk and JeffLion as they wander into an area of tall grass. SusieWitch makes a harsh comment when the screen image moves onto Larry. Larry looks confused as to where they need to go. Larry is looking all around then looks straight into the (lens) view of the crystal TV...Larry's face is distorted as he gets close to the camera lens (distortion filter - looking through a peephole on a door). Larry makes a comment about the 'ugly wicked witch'.

Larry (shown on crystal-TV screen): "I pity the poor bastard that marries that loudmouth witch."

SusieWitch (watching the crystal-TV): "LOUDMOUTH WITCH?? I'll fix you, my pretty...you four-eyed fuck. And your pussy friends too!"

JeffLion (shown on crystal-TV screen): "I'm starving. Can we go for an In-N-Out burger?"

Larry reaches in to the basket (feels around) and pulls out a large (pre-cut) sandwich.

JeffLion (shown on crystal-TV screen): "What kind of sandwich is that?"

Larry (shown on crystal-TV screen/examining the sandwich): "Don't know...looks like whitefish and cream cheese with onions and capers."

JeffLion (shown on crystal-TV screen): "Sounds delicious. Let's Eat."

Larry (shown on crystal-TV screen) hands a piece to JeffLion (along with a napkin), a piece to TinFunk and a piece to RichardCrow. Larry looks inside the basket (for another napkin).

Larry (shown on crystal-TV screen): "Can you believe this? Only one napkin!"

SusieWitch (watching the crystal-TV): "I'll fix all of you...Poison...Poison...POISON."

SusieWitch sprinkles poison dust over the crystal-TV. The poison dust falls from the sky onto the sandwich (seen on crystal-TV) Larry, RichardCrow, TinFunk and JeffLion are about to eat.

SusieWitch (watching the crystal-TV): "Sleep, you morons, sleeeeeeeep."

The four of them take a bite and simultaneously/ immediately fall to the ground.

< SCENE TRANSITION >

Larry, RichardCrow, TinFunk and JeffLion are sleeping in a patch of tall grass. The sun is beginning to rise [camera pans past the sleeping group...and zooms out to reveal they are sleeping in a roadside memorial of flowers]. CherylWitch appears in a bubble (hovering over them).

CherylWitch: "My sweet Larry...poisoned by the wicked witch to sleep for all eternity."

CherylWitch (bubble has 'popped') moves close to Larry and gives him a kiss on the forehead. Larry awakens and sees CherylWitch.

Larry (groggy): "Shara...WAIT...WHAT? What happened?"

CherylWitch: "The wicked witch placed a spell on you. You only needed a sincere, loving kiss to awaken you."

Larry: "I'm still feeling a little sleepy. How about another?"

CherylWitch: "Larry! Who's Shara?"

Larry (gesturing to JeffLion, RichardCrow, and TinFunk): "Never mind. What about them?"

CherylWitch (back inside the bubble, floating away): "They need a sign of your kindness to awaken them."

Larry: "Ehhhhh...let 'em sleep."

Larry reaches in to the basket (feels around) and pulls out a styrofoam food container (marked 'Al Abbas Chicken') and begins eating a piece.

RichardCrow, TinFunk and JeffLion begin sniffing (facial expressions) as they sleep. The sniffing expressions become more exaggerated and they all wake up.

JeffLion: "What do you have there?"

Larry turns away and attempts to hide his chicken.

TinFunk (sniffing): "It's Al Abbas, isn't it?"

JeffLion: "I LOVE Al Abbas. It's chicken to die for!"

RichardCrow: "Hey. What the hell was in that sandwich?...RUFIES?"

Larry reaches in to the basket (feels around) and pulls out a handful of chicken drumsticks and gives them each one.

RichardCrow (waving a chicken drumstick): "You can pull a half a chicken out of that thing and not a single drink? Come on already, (belches) let's get the fuck out of here…"

Richard Lewis (stepping out of character, addressing the camera): "*What the fuck*? Can't I get a different line? Look at THIS? (Richard Lewis grabs an off-camera cue card and waves it at Larry.) It's the same *fucking* line over and over. Who's writing this shit? (Richard, looking at camera) Don't you dare turn that camera off. Keep rolling." (Resumes the RichardCrow character.)

Larry, RichardCrow, and TinFunk and JeffLion resume walking up the street/The Path of Stars.

9. EXT. THE WIZ' CASTLE – DAY (DREAM SEQUENCE)
(Walking along The Hollywood Walk of Fame with a scene transition to the front of the Hollywood Castle).

Larry: "I see it. I SEE IT… there it is! It's the place of the Wiz!"

TinFunk (excited), begins to run-shuffle quickly towards the building (sounds of metal clanking as he moves). Larry, RichardCrow and JeffLion approach the giant front door. Using the door's oversized steel knocker, they knock loudly. The door porthole is opened by **WANDAGUARD (WANDA SYKES)**. (Audio dub: Loud, funky rap music is heard coming from inside the castle.)

WandaGuard: "Has the circus come to town? What in THE HELL do you want?"

Larry explains they need to see the Wiz to request he grant them some wishes.

Larry: "I need to get home, JeffLion needs balls, TinFunk wants some spunk and..."

WandaGuard interrupts Larry.

WandaGuard: "You must be mistakin' the Wiz for Santa Claus. Next, you and your freak show will want to sit on his lap, have cookies and milk, and ask for gifts."

WandaGuard slams the porthole door in his face. Larry looks at his friends and their disappointed faces, turns around and knocks again (louder/harder). The porthole is again opened by WandaGuard.

WandaGuard: "Get the hell off the property before I turn the dogs on you. And let me ask you somethin'...what's with the girlie basket?"

Larry reaches into the basket (feels around) and pulls out a handful of Oreo cookies. The cookies are separated and the white cookie filling has been eaten. WandaGuard notices the cookies have no filling and accuses Larry of being racist.

WandaGuard: "WHAT in the hell is the matter with you? You're too good for the BLACK part of the cookie? Is THAT it? You a cookie racist, eating all the white stuff and leavin' the black behind."

WandaGuard's attention is diverted and she looks upward towards the sky.

WandaGuard (continues looking upward): "Which one of you is the Four-Eyed Fuck?"
TinFunk, RichardCrow, and JeffLion all point at Larry. Larry turns around and looks/glares at them as they point at him. TinFunk, RichardCrow, and JeffLion begin looking upward at the sky. [Camera angle pulls back to reveal SusieWitch riding a broom and skywriting a phrase].
As everyone looks up, TinFunk, RichardCrow, and JeffLion read the skywriting (out loud/in unison).

TinFunk, RichardCrow, and JeffLion:

Surrender Larry,
You bald-headed
Four-eyed fuck!

WandaGuard: "You need to take your racist cookies, your freak show clan and get the hell out of here."

Larry puts the cookie remnants back in the basket. He feels around and then pulls out and displays the scroll-note (*from Scene 2*).

"Follow the Path of Stars and ye shall find the Wiz. Stray not from the path and beware of the wicked witch..."

WandaGuard: "Well, why didn't you show that in the first place...(voice trailing off) dumbass."

WandaGuard opens the door and lets them in. WandaGuard takes them through the castle to the Great Room. WandaGuard announces their presence (to the Wiz) and leaves. A 'floating' image of LeonWiz is seen through smoke and fire. LeonWiz is hitting on a woman (woman's face not seen onscreen).

LeonWiz: "mmmmm...delicious, I'm gonna do my DIZZLE after I get rid of these losers..."

(Audio dub – off-screen woman: "But you promised to topsy turvy me.")

JeffLion: "Who talks like that?"

LeonWiz turns and looks into the camera lens ('double take'/looks twice) and realizes the camera is broadcasting him ('live').

LeonWiz (looking into the camera): "I'm THE WIZ with THE DIZ. What the fuck!...Halloween's over. Who are you and what do you want?"

Larry explains their journey. LeonWiz asks Larry about the others with him.

LeonWiz (pointing to TinFunk): "What's up with this junk yard?...", (points at RichardCrow), "and the drunk?", (points at JeffLion), "and the big pussy?"

TinFunk, RichardCrow and JeffLion are nervous/frightened. One at a time, they each ask the Wiz for their wish.

LeonWiz (to Larry): "And what's with you, Mister Rogers with your girlie basket. What do you want?"

Larry tells LeonWiz he just wants to go home.

LeonWiz: "You got someone to go home to?"

Larry: "Nah...no one special...just a mooch I can't get rid of."

LeonWiz tells them he will grant their wishes but first they must prove themselves worthy. LeonWiz tells them they must bring him something from the wicked witch.

LeonWiz: "Go to the wicked witch's tower and bring me...the head. (Voice roaring) BRING ME THE HEAD OF THE JUDY DOLL."

[Audio dub/off camera] **Woman's voice**: "Come on Wiz, time for your DIZ."

A woman's hand is seen reaching for LeonWiz, grabbing him. LeonWiz turns to look at her. LeonWiz turns the camera off and his floating image fades out.

Larry and TinFunk agree to go to the wicked witch's tower and retrieve the head. JeffLion doesn't want to go and RichardCrow objects as well.

Larry: "It's no big deal. We'll just zip in and zip out."

RichardCrow: "For fucks sake. My feet hurt. You been leading us on this never-ending walk...the pilgrimage to Mecca would be shorter! And now you want to *visit* some psychotic broom-flying bitch from hell and steal her doll head? HOW fucked up does THAT sound. And I'm supposed to be the raging drunk in this cluster fuck?"

Larry (bewildered by the insults) reaches into the basket (feels around) and pulls out a fortune cookie. He opens the cookie and looks at the fortune. He turns to RichardCrow.

Larry (to RichardCrow): "It's for you."

Larry hands the fortune to RichardCrow.

TinFunk: "What's it say?"

RichardCrow looks at the fortune.

RichardCrow (to Larry): "Fuck YOU."

TinFunk: "What's it say?"

RichardCrow hands the fortune to JeffLion. JeffLion reads it silently/to himself.

TinFunk: "What the hell? Has everyone taken a vow of silence? (yelling) WHAT'S IT SAY?"

JeffLion: "It says 'Jai-Ya'*. What's that mean?"

JeffLion tries to hand the fortune to TinFunk. TinFunk refuses to take the fortune and responds.

TinFunk: "You know what? Fuck you and your fortune."

JeffLion turns to Larry and tries to give him back the fortune. Larry refuses to take the fortune and responds.

Larry (sarcastic): "Fuck you."

JeffLion: "Jai-Ya! (yells) FUCK ME!" ('Fuck me' echoes loudly several times).

They all turn (simultaneously) and leave.

*-'Jai-Ya' was identified as Larry's mantra in Season 3, Episode 6 - The Special Section of Curb Your Enthusiasm. In the episode, he 'gave' the mantra to Richard Lewis and then had a change of heart and asked for it back. Richard Lewis (infuriated at the request to return it) discovered the (alleged) true meaning of the mantra ('fuck me') and throws it back in Larry's face.

10. EXT-INT. WATTS TOWER/SUSIEWITCH'S CASTLE – DAY (DREAM SEQUENCE)

Larry, JeffLion, TinFunk and RichardCrow approach SusieWitch's castle (Watts Tower). The castle door is closed. JeffLion pleads to turn back before it's too late. RichardCrow tells him to be quiet.

RichardCrow: "shhhhh! Why don't you just announce 'WE'RE HERE'? Maybe we should send that wicked bitch a telegram telling her we've come for the head."

TinFunk points out an open window above the door. Larry

suggests they lift someone up through the window.

RichardCrow: "Through the window? What are we, the Chinese acrobats from Shanghai?"

TinFunk: "Don't look at me. I'm too rusty for that."

Larry and TinFunk look at JeffLion.

JeffLion: "Seriously? You three twigs will need a crane to hoist my fat ass up there. I'm OUT."

Larry, TinFunk, and JeffLion turn and look at RichardCrow.

Larry (to RichardCrow): "RichieBOY…"

RichardCrow: "Ohhh. Fuck ME. I'm not doin' it. Absolutely not. No fucking way. I don't want you three schmucks pushing my balls up through my throat."

< SCENE TRANSITION >

Larry, TinFunk, and JeffLion struggle to lift RichardCrow up to the window.

RichardCrow: "I can't believe I let you fuckers talk me into this."

RichardCrow belches and (audio dub) passes gas as his backside is close to JeffLion's face.

RichardCrow: "Ahhhh fuck…it's be a sloppy one…"

JeffLion (disgusted by the reeking gas odor) lets go of

RichardCrow. JeffLion falls against the castle door. The door swings open with a loud creak (audio dub: creak). Larry and TinFunk wobble and RichardCrow slips to the ground.

RichardCrow: "You mean the door was open the WHOLE fucking time?...and you didn't think to try it first? ('under his breath') Fucking imbeciles."

They all walk in through the open door. The door 'automatically' slams behind them (audio dub: loud bang with echo).

TinFunk notices a suit of armor off to the side. He walks up to it and starts tinkering with it. The entire suit collapses with a loud crashing sound.

RichardCrow (to TinFunk): "Jesus FUCKING Christ!"

Larry & JeffLion (to TinFunk): "SHHHHH."

They walk through the entryway into a large room decorated in medieval style. Larry spots the Judy Doll head (displayed on a post inside a glass bell jar).

Larry: "There it is! JUDY!...it's Judy!"

Larry and JeffLion exchange 'high fives'.
Larry rushes over to the jar and lifts up the glass top.
When Larry removes the doll head from its post, bars slide down over the windows and across the doors, trapping them. JeffLion (scared) runs to a corner of the room, faces the wall and whimpers. Larry takes the head and places it in the basket.

TinFunk: "Look what you've done now, Larry."

SusieWitch and the winged monkey **ANDYMONKEY**
(**RICHARD KIND**) appear from a cloud of smoke.
(Audio dub music track: opening bars of 'For whom the bell
tolls' by Gianni Ferrio.)

Larry, RichardCrow, TinFunk and JeffLion
(simultaneously): "Oh, Shit."

SusieWitch: "Seize them. SEIZE them!"

AndyMonkey looks around as if to see who she's speaking
to.

SusieWitch (to Larry): "I'll fix you. I'll fix ALL of you..."

RichardCrow (to Larry): "What's your plan NOW, genius?"

Larry reaches into the basket (feels around) and pulls out
the Rat Dog, holding it in his arm. The Rat Dog barks at
SusieWitch.

SusieWitch: "And your mangy little Rat Dog too."

Larry pushes the Rat Dog back into the basket.
SusieWitch looks past Larry and sees the empty glass jar
that held the Judy Doll head.

SusieWitch: "Where's my doll head?? WHERE'S MY
FUCKING DOLL HEAD?"

Larry is scratching his crotch.

SusieWitch (shouting): "Quit scratching your balls, you sick perverted asshole, and give me the doll head. GIVE ME THE HEAD."

RichardCrow (to Larry/mocking SusieWitch): "Yeah, quit scratching your balls and give her the head you sick perverted asshole."

SusieWitch (to RichardCrow): "You keep your mouth shut. One more word from you and I'll shove a cocktail umbrella up your ass and use your empty skull as a martini shaker."

Larry opens the basket [camera close up into basket] and discovers it's empty. Larry pauses for a moment, reaches into his pants and extracts the doll head."

SusieWitch (screaming): "You freak of fucking nature. What is that?...Some kind of voodoo shit? I'll FIX YOU."

SusieWitch 'conjures up' a ball of fire and 'throws' it at Larry. Larry steps out of the way of its path and it hits RichardCrow. RichardCrow's shirt sleeve catches fire. RichardCrow waves his burning arm franticly and backs up attempting to put out the fire. Larry jumps back (dropping the doll head), reaches into the basket (feels around) and pulls out a box of salt. He dumps the salt on RichardCrow's arm and puts the flames out. RichardCrow's sleeve is still smoking. Larry reaches into the basket again and pulls out an open bottle of club soda. RichardCrow sees the bottle and tells Larry he needs a drink and grabs for it. Larry and RichardCrow wrestle over the bottle of club soda. Larry yanks it away from RichardCrow, and in doing so sprays/douses SusieWitch with the club soda.

SusieWitch: "AHHHHHH...Look what you've done. I'm melting. I'm melting. What a world. What a world. Who would have thought a bald-headed prick could destroy my beautiful wickedness?"

SusieWitch melts into a pile of green slime on the floor.

JeffLion: sarcastic laugh

The bars over the windows and doors retract.

AndyMonkey glares at Larry.

Larry (offers bottle to AndyMonkey): "Club Soda?"

AndyMonkey: "You killed the wicked witch. You KILLED her."

Larry: "Are you sure she's dead?"

AndyMonkey: "She's a steaming pile of green slime...what do you think?"

Larry picks up the Judy doll head and puts it in the basket.

RichardCrow: "Come on already. (belches) Let's get the..."

Richard Lewis (stepping out of character, addressing the camera): "I'm not reading this fucking line again. Someone else read it."

TinFunk (squinting/looking at cue card): "Come...on

...al-rea-dy. (reads word) 'bel-ches'... Let's get...the...fuck out of here."

Larry: "Jesus...you don't need reading glasses, you need the Hubble telescope."

AndyMonkey: "I'm good. You go. (squinting/looking at cue card) You guys...get the...fuck out of here."

AndyMonkey pulls out a cell phone and takes several 'selfies' with the green pile of slime.

Larry, TinFunk, RichardCrow, and JeffLion turn (simultaneously) and leave.

11. EXT. RETURN TO THE WIZ'S CASTLE – DAY (DREAM SEQUENCE)

Larry, JeffLion, TinFunk and RichardCrow return to the Wiz's Castle. They approach the giant front door and knock loudly. The door port hole is opened by WandaGuard. [Audio dub: Loud, funky rap music coming from inside the castle.]

WandaGuard: "YOU again...still carrying that girlie basket. You got more racist cookies in there?"

Larry: "No cookies...but we have it. The Wiz told us to bring something back and we have it."

Larry reaches into the basket, (feels around) and pulls out the Rat Dog. The Rat Dog barks and nips at WandaGuard.

WandaGuard: "You brought a racist dog. You trained that dog to be racist, didn't you? Barkin' and shit at the black folk...You got a clan dog."

JeffLion leans in to look at the dog. The dog barks and nips at JeffLion. JeffLion backs up and hides behind TinFunk. The dog leaps from the basket and runs away.
Larry (defensive): "No. We didn't bring a clan dog."

Larry reaches into the basket again (feels around) and pulls out the Judy Doll head.

WandaGuard: "Well, why didn't you show that in the first place...(voice trailing off) dumbass."

WandaGuard opens the door and lets them in.

Larry, JeffLion, TinFunk and RichardCrow enter. Larry tells WandaGuard he needs to use the bathroom.

WandaGuard criticizes Larry's request.

WandaGuard: "Is that what you do?...you go to other people's castle's and use their bathroom? Why don't you go at home like a normal person?"

WandaGuard (shaking her head) points Larry down a hallway.

12. INT. THE HALL OF DOORS OF A DIFFERENT COLOR (INSIDE THE CASTLE) - DAY (DREAM SEQUENCE)

Larry enters The Hall of Doors of a Different Color (a long hallway filled with different colored doors). Larry goes from door to door (opening each) looking for the bathroom.

1.**Ted and Mary**: Larry approaches and opens a door. The setting inside is Ted and Mary's house. **TED DANSON** and **MARY STEENBURGEN** appear from behind the door.

Mary: "Larry? What are you doing here?"

Ted: "Larry, the party was last night."

Ted and Mary (reaching for Larry): "As long as you're already here, why don't you come in?"

Larry declines, pulling away from them, backing out and closing the door.

< SCENE TRANSITION >

2. **Auntie Rae**: Larry approaches the next door and opens it. **Auntie Rae** (**ELLIA ENGLISH**) is in the room and (excitedly) greets Larry. She reaches out and pulls Larry in for a hug. The hug lingers. After several seconds, Larry glances downward and displays a look of concern/anguish on his face. (Camera pans down to Larry's waist-area.) Auntie Rae pushes Larry away from her and stares at his crotch.

Auntie Rae: "Larry! That's disgusting."

Auntie Rae shoves Larry backwards through the open door and slams the door shut in his face.

< SCENE TRANSITION >

3. **Bill Buckner**: Larry approaches the next door and sees a baseball on the ground. He picks it up and opens the door. **BILL BUCKNER** is standing inside, holding a baseball mitt.

Larry (to Bill): "You ready Buck? You ready? Gonna put a little heat on it."

Larry tosses the baseball at Bill. The ball takes a bounce off the floor and goes through Bill's legs.

Bill Buckner: "That was a horseshit throw, Larry."

Larry: "I thought you were a professional!"

Bill Buckner: "Horseshit throw!"

Larry: "It WASN'T a horseshit throw...it was a horseshit catch."

Larry backs up, closing the door, repeating 'horseshit catch' as Bill is repeating 'horseshit throw'.

< SCENE TRANSITION >

4. **Chef Guy Bernier**: Larry approaches the next door and opens it. **Chef Guy Bernier** (**PAUL SAND**) is in the room, set like a kitchen, chopping the head off a salmon with a cleaver. He looks up/notices Larry.

Chef Guy: "Bonsoir!...FUCKHEAD, SHITFACE, COCKSUCKER, ASSHOLE, SONOFABITCH, SALMON."

Larry (backing up, reaching for the door): "SCUM SUCKING MOTHER FUCKING WHORE." (Larry shuts the door.)

< SCENE TRANSITION >

5. **Mr. Takahashi**: Larry approaches the next door, opens it, and is immediately confronted by **Mr. Takahashi** (**DANA LEE**).

Mr. Takahashi (in Larry's face): "YOU! YOU KILL BLACK SWAN!"

Larry repeatedly performs a very shallow bow. While backing up, he replies.

Larry (reaching for the door): "So sorry. So sorry."

Mr. Takahashi yells at Larry.

Mr. Takahashi: "YOU KILL BLACK SWAN! And you give shit bow. SHIT BOW...SHIT BOW..." (as Larry shuts the door.)

< SCENE TRANSITION >

6. **Bam Bam:** Larry approaches the next door, opens it slightly and pauses. From inside (unseen), the voice of **Bam Bam Funkhouser** (**Catherine O'Hara**) is heard.

Bam Bam: "Hey...Hey...ohhh...HEY. OHHH, fuck me fat boy, FUCK me, fat boy."

Larry immediately pulls the door closed (displaying a look of horror) and backs away from the door.

< SCENE TRANSITION >

7. **Rosie O'Donnell:** Larry approaches the next door and opens it. He is greeted by **ROSIE O'DONNELL**, wearing a neck brace.

Rosie: "Larry!"

Larry: "Neck brace??...Car accident?"

Rosie (irritated): "No!"

Rosie repeatedly clears her throat.

Larry: "Hair...in...throat?"

Rosie (pauses/irritated): "THAT'S RIGHT, Larry...Hair in throat."

Larry: "Hmmmm...neck brace...hair in throat..."

Rosie pushes Larry back through the open door and slams the door in his face.

< SCENE TRANSITION >

8. **Shara:** Larry approaches the next door and opens it. He is greeted by **Shara** (**ANNE BEDIAN**).

Shara: "Hello Labe...Son of Nat."

Larry: "Mmmm, let's leave my father out of this—he's no longer with us."

Shara: "Come, Larry...I will fuck the Jew out of you."

Larry takes a step back (outside of door) and pauses.

Shara: "Larry, my sister Jasmine is with me."

Larry shrugs, goes into the room and closes the door behind him (Camera shot remains on closed door. A video-graphic of clock, hands rapidly spinning, is superimposed over outside of door. The door opens (clock graphic disappears). Larry emerges from room, buttoning up his shirt and closes door behind him.

Larry: "Small price to pay...for the best sex ever."

< SCENE TRANSITION >

9. **Anna:** Larry approaches the next door and opens it. He is greeted by **ANNA**, the dry cleaner (**GINA GERSHON**).

Anna: "Hello, Larry...I heard you through the wall...you've been a busy boy. I'll have your semen covered blanket ready on Wednesday."

Larry pulls the door closed and backs away from the door.

< SCENE TRANSITION >

10. **DUCK SOUP**: Larry approaches the next door and opens it. The setting is a bathroom. Larry enters the bathroom and uses a urinal.

< SCENE TRANSITION >

Larry flushes the urinal and goes to the sink. As he is washing his hands, he is startled by a **bathroom attendant (BOB WEIDE)**. The bathroom attendant greets Larry and offers him an array of bathroom supplies. Larry looks over the supplies and notices a long loaf of Italian bread. Larry is perplexed.

Bathroom Attendant: "Say...can I ask a quick favor? I need to drop the kids off at the pool...you know...take the browns to the superbowl. Can you cover for me and watch the supplies? Just take a New York minute."

Without waiting for an answer, the Bathroom Attendant enters a stall and shuts the door. Larry looks at himself in the mirror and looks/checks his teeth in the reflection. Larry looks down at the basket of supplies and retrieves a container of dental floss. Larry looks back up to the mirror. Larry's reflection has been replaced with the bathroom attendant in makeup, to (almost) resemble Larry. Larry shakes his head and rubs his eyes and face. The bathroom attendant 'reflection' mimics Larry's gestures and movements. Larry pauses. The bathroom attendant 'reflection' pauses. Larry touches his neck. The bathroom attendant 'reflection' touches his own neck. Larry leans forward, backward, and side to side. The bathroom attendant 'reflection' leans forward, backward, and side to side with a slight lag to Larry's movements. Larry reaches up with his hand to touch the 'mirror'. The bathroom attendant 'reflection' reaches up with his hand to touch Larry's hand. Larry performs a 360-degree spin (circle) and ends with his arms outstretched. The bathroom attendant 'reflection' does not spin, but stretches out his arms to mimic Larry's.

A loud toilet flush noise is heard and Larry looks towards the stall. When he turns to look back at the 'mirror', the bathroom attendant 'reflection' has been replaced with Larry's true reflection. The bathroom attendant exits the stall.

Larry (to attendant): "Were you just…"
Larry looks back and forth at the mirror and the attendant.

Larry walks up to the bathroom attendant and does the 'Lie-Eye-Stare'.

Larry: "OK."

Bathroom Attendant (offering to Larry): "Mint?"

Larry leaves the room, closing the door behind him.

< SCENE TRANSITION >

11. A tail of two Wandas: Larry approaches and opens a door that leads back to the entryway where he left TinFunk, JeffLion and RichardCrow. Larry is looking directly at Wanda/WandaGuard's backside. Larry steps through the doorway.

< SCENE TRANSITION – return to castle entryway >

Larry: "I'd know that tush anywhere."

WandaGuard: (insulted/turns to face Larry): "Is that how you say hello? Are you some kinda big ass freak? You a big ass man…is that it?"

< SCENE TRANSITION >

WandaGuard takes Larry, JeffLion, TinFunk and
RichardCrow to the Great Room to see the Wiz.

WandaGuard (warning Larry): "The Wiz is an ass man like
you Larry, so I'm tellin' you, I wouldn't turn my back to the
Wiz."
WandaGuard leaves. A 'floating' image of LeonWiz is seen
through the smoke and fire. LeonWiz is hitting on a woman
(woman's face not seen onscreen). LeonWiz turns and
looks into the camera lens ('double take'/looks twice) and
realizes the camera is broadcasting him ('live').

LeonWiz (video image): "You back already? Did you prove
yourselves worthy and get the shit?"

Larry: "We got it...we got THE SHIT."

Larry reaches into the basket (feels around), pulls out the
Judy Doll head and holds it towards the floating image of
LeonWiz.

Larry: "We brought you the Judy head, as you
requested...and now, we'd like our wishes."

LeonWiz tries to renege on his promise to grant them their
wishes.

(A man's voice is heard off camera). **Man's voice**: "HEY.
What are you doing? QUIT SCREWING AROUND WITH MY
GEAR."

A commotion takes place behind a curtain off to the side of

the room. The curtain pulls back revealing LeonWiz struggling with the real Wiz, **MELWIZ(MEL BROOKS**) over the controls for the 'floating image' camera. They stop struggling (surprised expressions) and turn to look at Larry, TinFunk, RichardCrow and JeffLion.

Larry (holding the head of the Judy Doll approaches MelWiz and LeonWiz): "What's going on here and who are you?"

MelWiz: "I'm the genuine Wiz. I'm sorry you had to see this ruckus. I told him not to mess with my gear while I was out getting a burger (displays a bag of In-N-Out)."

JeffLion: "I LOVE that place...did you get the chocolate shake too?"

Larry: "So you're the real Wiz (Larry does 'Lie-Eye-Stare' with MelWiz)...OK...then who the hell is he (pointing at LeonWiz)?"

MelWiz: "He's the parking valet...which reminds me (turns to LeonWiz), you pig parked THAT Prius in my spot again. GO MOVE IT."

LeonWiz: "You mean, like, right now?"

MelWiz (to Larry): "Can you believe this guy?"

MelWiz (to LeonWiz): "YES, NOW!"

MelWiz (to Larry): "Let me ask you something? What's with the doll head (gesturing at the Judy Doll head)?"

Larry: "We brought it back to prove our worthiness so THAT Wiz (points to LeonWiz) would grant us our wishes. We had to liquidate the wicked witch to get the head."

MelWiz tells them they didn't have to prove themselves at all and he would have granted their wishes at any time.
RichardCrow: "So the whole trip was a fucking waste of time. Nice, Larry. NICE."

TinFunk: "You really fucked us over, Larry. I have metal shards up my rectum from plodding along this fucked up Path of Stars...and how many Stars did we see? Not one. Not a single one."

MelWiz: "Everyone calm down and I'll grant each of your wishes. If we're through kibitzing...what is it that each of you want?"

One at a time, TinFunk, RichardCrow and JeffLion each tell the Wiz what they are wishing for.

MelWiz (to Larry): "And you, my bald-headed friend, what do you want?"

Larry tells MelWiz he just wants to go home.

MelWiz: "Ahhhh, there's someone you want to go home to?"

Larry: "Nah...no one special...just a mooch I can't get rid of."

MelWiz: "**LOL**, Larry. **LOL**."

Larry: "Really? Couldn't you just *laugh* out loud?"

MelWiz ignores the comment and turns to RichardCrow.

MelWiz: "So…you asked for a drink?"

RichardCrow: "Gonna take more than one after travelling with these schmucks."
MelWiz holds up a remote control, presses a button and a curtain retracts revealing a fully stocked bar. MelWiz holds up a small picnic cooler (labeled, 'Medical – Organ Transplants') and offers it to RichardCrow.

MelWiz: "You probably would like a new liver to go with that (pointing to the bar), but we're fresh out of livers right now…however, I can offer you this kidney (hands the organ-cooler to RichardCrow)."

RichardCrow runs to the bar holding the kidney-cooler.

RichardCrow: "Daddy's COMING!"

MelWiz turns to TinFunk.

MelWiz: "And you, my overgrown corroded comrade, you wanted spunk…and SPUNK you shall have."

MelWiz pulls a long fanfold strip of blue pills from his coat pocket.

MelWiz (to TinFunk): "Just take one of these little Vitamin V pills and you'll have spunk for 24 hours. (MelWiz looks TinFunk up and down). Maybe take two."

TinFunk immediately swallows three.

TinFunk: "I have a lot of rust to blow out, if you know what I'm saying. The SPUNKMAN's BACK!"

JeffLion: "What about ME?"

MelWiz (to JeffLion): "Ah, yes, you, my chunky amigo... Let's see, you wanted..."

JeffLion: "BALLS! I WANT BALLS. GIVE ME A SET OF BALLS."

MelWiz: "Of course. And balls you will get. (MelWiz reaches into his coat pocket and pulls out two baseballs). Here's your set of balls --- two genuine Mookie Wilson autographed baseballs (MelWiz hands the balls to JeffLion)."

JeffLion: "I LOVE Mookie Wilson."

MelWiz: "Of course...BUT WAIT, there's MORE!"

MelWiz retrieves a large/full bag from In-N-Out Burger and holds it out to JeffLion. JeffLion grabs it from MelWiz and turns away. [Audio dub: paper ripping sounds].

MelWiz turns to Larry.

MelWiz (to Larry): "And last, but not least...You, my friend, you could have gone home anytime you wanted. You only needed to set things right with those atrocious red shoes. You see, [pointing to shoes; camera close up] you have them on the wrong feet –you have the left shoe on the right foot and the right shoe on the left. You only have to reverse them, click your heels together and say three times, 'there's no place like home', and home you will go."

Larry reverses the shoes/puts them on the correct feet. The shoes glow a brilliant red. Larry taps his heels together and repeats the instruction.

Larry: "There's no place like home, there's no place like home..." (Larry pauses and turns to MelWiz).

Larry: "Wiz. Wizzo. Wizman. Let me ask you something? There's one little thing...if you could do me a small favor. There was this hot...bubbly, blonde I met...Glin...Glenlivet or Glenfiddich, or some damn thing--I just called her Cheryl..."

MelWiz (smiling): "Ahhhh, sure...Glinda-Anastasia-Cordelia-Cherylesque-Daveedess, the good witch. She certainly has a great bubble."

Larry: "Could you put in a good word for me?...That's someone I could be with NOW and for ALL eternity."

MelWiz: "Really? For ALL eternity?"

MelWiz gives Larry the 'Lie-Eye-Stare'.

MelWiz: "...mmm, OK. I'll see what I can do."
Larry turns to JeffLion, TinFunk and RichardCrow. Larry motions with the basket to RichardCrow.

Larry: "This is yours now."

RichardCrow: "I don't want your pansy-ass lunchbox--- you'll probably want it back anyway."

RichardCrow shakes Larry's hand. Larry has (secretly) placed the 'Jai-Ya' fortune strip (from Scene 9) in his hand and transfers it to RichardCrow's hand as they shake. RichardCrow pulls his hand back and looks at the paper strip.

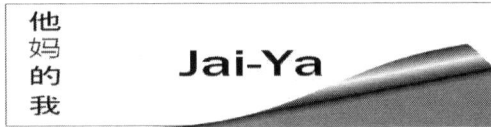

他
妈
的
我
Jai-Ya

RichardCrow: "Fuck me."

Larry says goodbye to TinFunk and JeffLion.

TinFunk: "How can I ever repay you...if you weren't leaving so soon, I would introduce you to my sister, Bam-Bam...she's SOOOOO special."

JeffLion (burger bun bits and french fries stuck to his face): "You my friend are going to a better place...a place where I'm BANNED...but maybe I can pop in and out sometime?"

Larry: "Ehhhh, I don't want you popping in...once you pop in, you can't just pop out...I'm ready to go home."

Larry repeats the instruction for a third time.

Larry: "There's no place like home."

A large cloud of smoke surrounds Larry. As the smoke clears, Larry is STILL standing there, coughing and waving away the smoke. Larry gestures at the Wiz. The Wiz throws an object at Larry's feet and another cloud of smoke billows up. Larry disappears.

13. INT. LARRY'S BEDROOM – DAY (TWO) NON DREAM SEQUENCE

[Scene is reset to regular/standard color/hues.]
Larry's Bedroom – Jeff, Susie, Funkhouser, Richard Lewis, Wanda, Ted, Mary, and Sammi are all standing around Larry's bed. Leon is standing in front of an open window. Susie puts a (steaming) hot towel on Larry's forehead (a raised purple bruise is visible).
Larry is moving his head and talking in his sleep-mumbling "too hot...too hot...too...too much mayo, too much mayo...No place like home, No place like home".

The crowd parts and Cheryl approaches Larry. She sits on the edge of the bed, removes the hot towel and gives Larry a kiss on the lips. Larry is motionless and silent.
(Audio dub: Mister Softee ice-cream truck music is heard through the open window.)

Larry awakens from his deep sleep. Larry (confused/looking around the room) sees everyone standing over him (everyone talking at the same time). They all stop and look at Larry.

Jeff: "Hey, pal. We thought you were gonna leave us forever."

Wanda: "Not that we minded."

Leon: "You remember me, don't you LD?"

Larry (sniffing): "What smells like strawberries and cotton candy?"

Leon: "You been dreamin' 'bout Latisha?"

Larry: "Latisha...(confused expression)...Strawberry shortcake?"

Leon: "Yup. She's using your shower to freshen up. She'll be out in a minute."

Larry (still confused) tells them about his dream recollections and that each of them played a part in his dream. Larry tells them that he was wearing magic red shoes. Larry checks under the sheets to see if his ruby red shoes are still on.

Larry (Looking around the room and notices Wanda, facing away from him): "Is *that* Wanda?"

Wanda (turning around to face Larry): "LD, are you saying 'Hello, BIG-ASS'?"

Ted/Mary: "You just had a bad dream, Larry."

Larry: But it wasn't a dream. It was a place...a real place. And you (pointing at Susie) were there...and (pointing at each one in succession) Jeff, and Marty and Wanda...and Leon...you were all there. Larry offends each of them as he explains their part.

Larry looks at each person in the room and tells everyone how special they are and how much they mean to him and that's he's NEVER going to leave again because there really is *No Place Like Home.*

Cheryl (with tears in her eyes) tightly embraces Larry on the bed. Cheryl says they were always meant to be together.

Cheryl (sitting up): "I love you Larry, always and unconditionally...NOW and through ALL eternity."

Larry reaches out and takes one of Cheryl's hand's as he gazes into her eyes. Gradually, Larry slides his other hand up to one of Cheryl's breasts. Cheryl looks down at Larry's hand on her chest.

Cheryl (annoyed expression): "You're NOT doing what I think you're doing?"

Larry: "Too soon?"

Larry slowly pulls his hand away from Cheryl's chest.

Susie: "LAR...don't you have SOMETHING to say to Cheryl?"

Larry (looking at Cheryl, awkward pause): "And I love...all of you...and there's no place like home."

Sammi (singing) breaks into 'Over the Rainbow' and everyone turns to look at her.

Sammi: "Somewhere over the rainbow, Way up high, And the dreams that you dreamed of, Once in a lullaby. Somewhere over the..." As Sammi begins the second verse, Larry interrupts and cuts her off.

Larry: "Alright. VERY GOOD. Thanks. Songs over. Give her a hand."

Everyone turns back towards Larry, yelling (in anger): "**LARRY**!" (Susie heard cursing, Lewis heard yelling, 'SCHMUCK').

[Camera shot lingers on Larry's face. Aperture-camera close.]

Cue Music.*

(END)

[* - We were at 'odds' over the last scene/ending. We originally wrote a very sparse, fast-paced ending. Then, we started tweaking it and it grew in size and complexity. Eventually, John turned back to the original ending of the Wizard of Oz movie and wanted to end this episode/scene here (using the OVER the Rainbow song and proving that Larry would ALWAYS be Larry). Ray was in favor of one final 'hook'—a crossover of sorts, taking a snippet from the dream sequence and reproducing it in the final scene. Since we couldn't decide, we wrote both. Thus, we offer an 'alternate' ending.]

Alternate Ending

Larry (awkward pause): "And I love......all of you...and there's no place like home."

Sammi (singing) breaks into 'Over the Rainbow' and everyone turns to look at her.

Sammi: "Somewhere over the rainbow, Way up high, And the dreams that you dreamed of, Once in a lullaby. Somewhere over the..." As Sammi begins the second verse, Larry interrupts and cuts her off.

Larry: "Alright. VERY GOOD. Thanks. Songs over. Give her a hand."

Everyone turns back towards Larry, yelling (in anger): "**LARRY**!" (Susie heard cursing, Lewis heard yelling, 'SCHMUCK').

Larry displays a perplexed expression. He looks down into his hand and notices a small scrap of paper. Larry unfolds it and reads it to himself. The camera angle reverses to Larry's point of view, revealing the words on the scrap of paper:

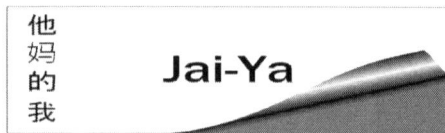

他
妈
的   Jai-Ya
我

[Camera shot returns and lingers on Larry's face/looking directly into the camera. Aperture-camera close.]

Cue Music.

(END)

22

BUT WAIT! THERE'S MORE! VOLUME 3?

Or *IS* there? Season 9 of Curb Your Enthusiasm finished filming in early April of 2017. We (Ray and John) had the privilege of being on the set and appearing in a restaurant scene in the final Episode (#10) of Season 9. (Watch for Ray sitting across from a stunning blonde at a table behind Larry and Jeff and John walking past Larry's table as they wait to order.)

For those that aren't up-to-date, it's been a five-year hiatus between seasons. A few weeks after Season 9 finished shooting, the entire season's episodes went in for editing. One of the peculiarities of Curb Your Enthusiasm is that each episode is not always filmed to conclusion. Scenes—mostly filler shots for an episode may be filmed as part of a later episode and edited in (as was the case for the outside-restaurant scenes shot in Season 9 - Episode 10 that turns up in Episode 2).

The BIG question, once again, is, WILL THERE BE MORE? Does Larry David want to do another season? Of course he 'has' another season in him, but it's a question of want. Will he? Won't he? Will it be another six years? The answers are only known to Larry David, but we can offer the following observations and thoughts.

One of the interesting aspects (to us) of the upcoming Season 9 is the use of cameo and guest-star appearances. While Curb Your Enthusiasm has always made use of interesting guest-stars, Season 9 took a potentially unfavorable turn with their use. Many of the guest-stars are 'returns' – they appeared in a previous episode or season of Curb and were brought back to recreate their role for an episode in Season 9. The recreation of past guest-star roles also coincided with revival of certain past plot lines (think: Chicken). This was a somewhat unexpected turn. Some close to the production company have suggested the cameos were a way to do a review

/retrospective of the entire series—making a goodwill gesture to those that previously appeared while tying up loose ends to previous story lines and bringing closure to the series.

Still...'closure' is a touchy subject with Larry David. The 2013 film, Clear History, was privately referred to as 'Curb: THE Movie' (See Chapter 20 for more on a possible Curb movie). Unfortunately, it wasn't well received. It didn't have the pace or humor of a Curb episode and generally was thought to be below Larry's usual standards. Does that rule out another Curb movie? Not at all. Or perhaps an occasional/one-off episode of Curb will appear. Or possibly an animated series. Or maybe a spinoff, as HBO is already talking about readying a replacement, should Curb in fact come to an end.

Another consideration is the cast themselves. A most recent and sad development was the death of actor-comedian Shelley Berman. Berman played Larry's father Nat in 15 episodes of Curb Your Enthusiasm. Another occasional guest on the show, Paul Mazursky who played the character of Norm, passed away in 2014. At the other end of the spectrum is Ashly Holloway, the actress that has played Sammi Greene in the series since 2001. Ashly can no longer act the part of a 'kid' role in the series, as will play out in Season 9 when her 'status' changes significantly. (Hint: Read Guys & Dolls / Chapter 7 again.)

Season 9 of Curb Your Enthusiasm remained in an 'unknown' status until filming actually started in November of 2016. Expect the definite decision regarding Season 10 of Curb Your Enthusiasm to be announced no later than the day it begins shooting. For us (John and Ray), our future may depend on it---we're sitting on multiple seasons' worth of outrageous, offensive material. It would be a crime to 'kick it to the CURB' or for it to remain forever LOST...

FADE OUT/Cue Music.

John & Ray

Printed in Great Britain
by Amazon